Word Processing

An introduction

SECOND EDITION

Peter Flewitt

M

MACMILLAN

First edition 1980
Reprinted 1981 (twice), 1983, 1984
Second edition 1985

Published by
MACMILLAN EDUCATION LTD
Houndmills, Basingstoke, Hampshire RG21 2XS
and London
Companies and representatives
throughout the world

Printed in Great Britain by
Anchor Brendon Ltd,
Tiptree, Essex

British Library Cataloguing in Publication Data
Flewitt, Peter
Word Processing – 2nd ed.
1. Word processing – Equipment and supplies
I. Title
652'.5   Z52.4
ISBN 0–333–39348–1

Contents

List of illustrations

Author's note

Throughout the course of this book it is necessary at times to refer to the executive or dictator, and the typing staff by personal pronouns. Whilst I freely accept that typists, supervisors and executives may be of either sex, it would have made for extremely tedious reading to allow for either eventuality in every case. As a matter of convenience and for greater clarity, I have adopted the convention of referring to authors, executives and originators of text generally as 'he', and typists, word processor operators and supervisory staff as 'she'. I hope that this will prove acceptable to even my most militant readers.

Acknowledgements

The author wishes to express grateful thanks to:
Philips Business Equipment for permission to reproduce or freely adapt material from their instructional and promotional literature;
Linda Clague and Irene Geis for their help with the examples in Chapter 5;
His wife and family for putting up with him during the months when this was being written.

Foreword

If you are a computer buff, or a senior O & M consultant weighing up the pros and cons of shared-logic versus mainframe systems, do not bother reading any further – this book is not for you. It is simply an attempt to reduce the complex mystique of word processing in its widest sense to simple everyday terms which can be understood by teachers, by students, and in fact by anybody who needs to know about the basic principles of word processing without delving deeply into the complexities of microelectronics.

The reader will be a person who needs to relate the new computer-based technology to the structure and procedures of the commercial office, a person who needs to see the concept of word processing not as an end in itself, but as a means of communicating between human beings.

Since this book was first written in 1980, there have been a number of changes in the word-processing field, not least in the increased use of word-processing software packages on computers and microcomputers. This revised version has been broadened in scope to embrace the use of such packages, highlighting where possible the essential differences between the various systems. In education, most if not all of the major Examining bodies now have examinations in Word Processing or Information Processing. In revising the book, the author has tried to envisage the kind of question likely to be asked, and to provide satisfactory answers.

The introduction of word processors in increasing numbers, and the likely acceleration of this trend as prices fall, is bringing about a reappraisal of the training needs of young people about to enter business life. Teachers of office skills in particular are looking very closely at their methods and syllabuses to see whether or not they measure up to the demands of the new technology. Many of the basic skills will remain (if not for ever at least for some time to come) essential to the office worker. Knowledge of the English language will be as important as it ever was, spelling and punctuation even more so.

The advisability of teaching shorthand to all and sundry will need to be considered carefully in the light of local requirements. The skills of fast, accurate typing and audio-typing will be paramount. Additional skills may become necessary as new kinds of job emerge.

To those who will be involved at first hand in the changes which are taking place, and to those who will prepare others to take a place in the new-technology-based offices, it is hoped this book will be a useful introduction.

Introductory glossary

To help you in the early stages . . .

Here is a short list of possibly unfamiliar terms which you may come across in the introductory sections. A brief explanation is given here, all are fully explained within the text, and a fuller glossary of a hundred or so such terms is printed at the end of the book.

Building-blocks Standard paragraphs used to construct letters, contracts, etc., by keying-in coded numbers for each paragraph.

Command sequence The order in which keys have to be pressed to instruct the machine to carry out certain tasks.

Daisy-wheel The commonest form of word-processing printer, so called because the printing element looks like a daisy.

Digital code The reduction of all numbers, letters, symbols and instructions to a series of 1s and 0s.

Fully-blocked A style of typewriting where each line begins at the left-hand margin.

Image copier A machine which can produce a copy directly from electrical signals generated by a word processor or similar device.

Ink-jet A printer which operates by spraying ink on to the paper in the form of the letters.

Keyboarding The operation of (usually) a typewriter-style keyboard, using correct fingering and technique.

Line-printer A printer which prints the whole line at once, not character by character.

Phototypesetter A composing machine which produces camera-ready copy for printing by photographic methods.

Prestel An information service provided by the Post Office whereby information from a central computer can be received via telephone lines on a television screen.

VDU Visual (or Video) Display Unit – the television screen upon which the work appears as it is typed.

Work disk The disk upon which work is recorded for future use after it has been produced on the screen.

1 What is word processing?

Overall concept

Well to begin with, it isn't computing! You don't need to know anything about programming, or hexadecimal equivalents, or debugging or any of the other things that computer people love to talk about. If anything, it's an extension of typewriting. A good typist is far more likely to be at home with a word processor than is the most knowledgeable of data-processing managers.

Word processing to one person will mean churning out endless streams of standard letters with simple variations of name and address. To another it may mean a typewriter with a television screen which makes the job of correcting errors almost as easy as making them. To a third it may mean the end of the filing cabinet. To a fourth it may conjure up a vision of the whole process from the conception of an original thought by an executive to the eventual interpretation of that thought, perhaps after it has passed through many stages or processes, by another human being. To my mind the last is nearest the mark; the first three are only very small parts of the whole concept of communication that is word processing.

Information processing

Remembering that the entire purpose of any form of business communication is the imparting of information by one human being to another, let us look at the broad concept of information processing, shown diagrammatically in Figure 1.

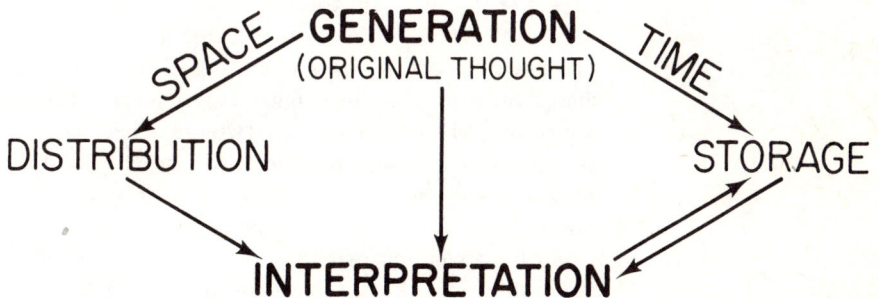

Fig 1 Information processes

Storage and distribution

We can see from this diagram that the original thought of the executive, author or originator may pass through many different processes. These may either *store* the information, thereby spanning *time* between conception and interpretation, or they may *distribute* or move the information over *distances* ranging from the other side of the desk to the other side of the Universe.

A *storage process* can be as simple as writing a message on the back of an old envelope, or as complicated as microfilming. *Distribution* can mean anything from passing a note hand to hand, to the facsimile reproduction of a document transmitted from a remote location by satellite. Here are a few examples of the two types of process:

STORAGE	DISTRIBUTION
Paper	*Physical*
Message pad	Person-to-person
Folder	Letter
Box file	Memo
Computer printout	Postal service
	Messenger
Text or data in digital form	
Floppy disk	*Electronic*
Hard, or rigid disk	Public telephone system
Microprocessor (silicon chip)	International telephone
Bubble memory	Public data network
Digital Optical Disk (laser disk)	Radio
	Telex
Text or data for reproduction	Communicating computers
Duplicating stencil	
Offset litho plate	
Camera-ready copy	
Sound	
Magnetic tape	
Record	
Laser disk	
Telephone answering machine	

I am sure that you can think of many more.

All of these processes have one thing in common; they should not in any way change the *content* of the original information. Looking back to Figure 1, we see that of all the processes implied, two are of necessity exclusive to human beings – the generation of original information, and its eventual interpretation. This may not necessarily be true in other fields such as computer-controlled machinery, where the wishes of a human programmer may be interpreted in the form of *action* by a welding machine, or capstan lathe. In our field, that of business communication, the only end-product is the passing of information from one human being to another. Between the two functions of generation and interpretation, many of the processes of storage and distribution can be taken over by machines.

The dictation machine, for example, can store the original text until such time as is convenient for the typist to transcribe it. Facsimile transmission, in which the image of a document is transmitted along a telephone line and reconstituted at the other end in its original form, can be the means of conveying a visual concept from one person to another.

The word processor may be a dedicated machine designed specifically for the purpose or a microcomputer using a word-processing software package and can encompass both storage and distribution. It can store information, ranging from simple business letters to comprehensive personnel records. Material thus stored can be recalled at any time to be merely consulted in the form of a display on a video screen, to be printed out as it stands, or to be edited, updated, changed or merged with new material to form new text. The more powerful machines can search their files for information, sort lists into alphabetical or numerical order, or perform complex arithmetical calculations. Some can even draw lines, and so can be used to produce forms, charts or simple diagrams.

As a means of distributing information, word processors can communicate with each other, with computers, with television-based information services such as the Post Office's Prestel, with Telex and Teletex terminals, with phototypesetters, and with image copiers which can produce copies directly from electrical signals. It is no longer necessary to entrust one's urgent business communication to the postal service. Matter produced on a word processor in the sender's office can be transmitted over telephone lines or specially-constructed data networks. It can then be printed out in the office of the recipient, within minutes of its having been dictated.

Conversion to machine language

Human beings communicate with words. Machines have their own language, which is called 'digital code'. Before information can be processed by electronic means, the words of which it consists must be converted into this digital code by means of a keyboard. Figure 2 shows this in a simplified form.

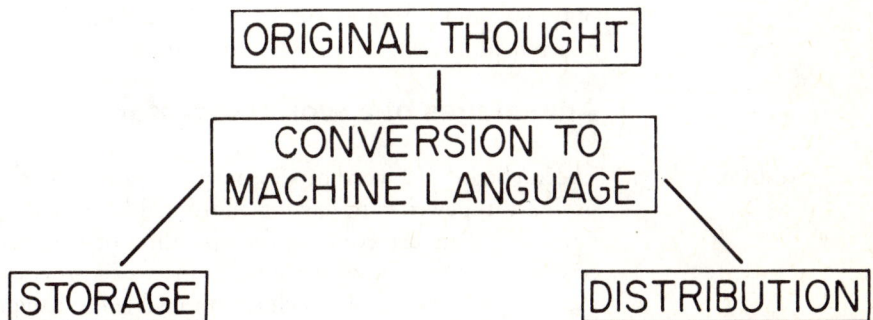

```
        ┌─────────────────────────┐
        │    ORIGINAL THOUGHT      │
        └─────────────┬───────────┘
        ┌─────────────┴───────────┐
        │     CONVERSION TO        │
        │    MACHINE LANGUAGE      │
        └──/───────────────────\──┘
    ┌───────────┐         ┌──────────────┐
    │  STORAGE  │         │ DISTRIBUTION │
    └───────────┘         └──────────────┘
```

Fig 2   Conversion to machine language

There are exceptions to this rule. Text may be typewritten, printed or occasionally handwritten, which may be read by a machine. This is called Optical Character Recognition. Some OCR machines require the use of special typefaces called OCR fonts, similar to the figures which you will see on cheques or credit cards. Others are capable of reading normal typewritten or printed material. The time approaches when the human voice will provide an acceptable input to a word processor. The technology exists, but at the time of writing the amount of memory capacity required to store speech in digitalised form precludes its use for dictation. It is increasingly used for command purposes, where it is only necessary for the machine to recognise relatively few words in order to call up text, or perform certain functions. For the time being however, the keyboard – and more importantly the person who uses it with skill and understanding – plays a vital part as the essential means of communication between man and machine.

The keyboard

This keyboard is probably the biggest anomaly that you are likely to encounter. It is our old friend QWERTY – the keyboard which was invented around 1873 to *slow down* the typist in order to prevent the typebars on the early typewriters from jamming together. Attempts have been made over the years to introduce newer, more efficient keyboards. These have been based on scientific principles of the frequency of use of letters and groups of letters, with attempts to balance the work of the two hands. It is ironic that the most frequently-quoted of these revised keyboards, the Dvorak, was patented in 1932 – the year of the first automatic typewriter. If only the one had enjoyed the success of the other, we would not now be employing a keyboard which was designed to slow down the typist, on machines which are intended to speed her up!

Another notable essay at redesigning the keyboard was by Lillian Malt. While Dvorak's efforts consisted of simply rearranging the keys in the usual four straight rows, Mrs Malt introduced ergonomic considerations by shaping the keyboard and varying the height of the keys in relation to the shape of the hand. Praiseworthy though these efforts were, both were doomed to failure by the commercial impracticability of changing from an established layout. Over the years more typewriters have come into use, and more typists have been trained to use them. To introduce a new keyboard today would involve retraining millions of typists, and scrapping similar numbers of machines. It seems that QWERTY will remain as long as a keyboard continues to be necessary.

Advantages of a word-processor

Additional keys The keyboard of a word processor or microcomputer may differ from that of an ordinary typewriter by having additional keys. These are known as 'function keys' and their use controls the operation of many of the complex functions possible on this type of machine. Some word processors have a great many of these keys, each one of which is responsible for a single function. On others, a proliferation of keys is avoided by the use of mnemonics. In this case, certain of the letters on the QWERTY keyboard are made to act as function keys when used as part of a 'command sequence' – that is, the order in which the keys are depressed in order to achieve a certain result. For example, on some systems the letter 'j' when incorporated into the 'print' command will cause the document to be printed with a justified right-hand margin. Similarly, as you will see when we come to consider command sequences in more detail later in the book, 'p' can mean paragraph or pitch according to the way in which it is used, 'w' is word, 'u' is underline, and so on.

Computers using word-processing software often use the QWERTY keys in conjunction with a CONTROL key to produce certain codes which the machine recognises as commands. On earlier software packages this often caused problems in that the operator needed to learn a series of keystroke combinations which as often as not bore no relation to the operation intended. It is now commonplace that many microcomputers have a number of 'spare' keys which can be programmed as function keys, thus bringing the equipment closer to the 'user-friendliness' of the dedicated systems.

Helping the typist   Without wishing to pre-empt the detailed accounts of some of the functions given in later chapters, let us look briefly at some of the ways in which this keyboard and its associated equipment can make the life of the typist very much easier.

If you were to ask a representative selection of typists to tell you the jobs which they hated most, it would be surprising if centring and margin justification did not rank high on the list. Right-hand margin justification, that is the production of text in which every line finishes precisely at the right-hand margin as on the printed page, is a time-consuming and soul-destroying task. Almost invariably the whole job has to be typed twice; once in order to count the number of spaces left at the end of each line, and then a second time to distribute those spaces between the words on the line so as to finish typing exactly at the margin. On a word processor all you need to do, is to modify the 'print' command slightly and the whole job is done automatically for you. Centring is another dreaded task, involving either counting the characters of each line, or backspacing from the centre of the page for each line. On a word processor the whole piece to be centred is simply typed on the screen in fully-blocked style and a simple command will centre the text either between the margins or around a point such as the cursor or a specified character-position. Some word processors will centre entire pages with one command, others need to have each line centred as a separate operation.

Ease of insertion   Many typists, particularly those engaged in more involved tasks such as lengthy reports or proposals, find that they spend much of their time retyping entire documents *through no fault of their own*. No typist can justifiably object to having to retype because she herself has committed some major error (usually towards the end of a long page!). She may however feel somewhat aggrieved when she has to rework whole pages to fit in some last-minute insertion at the whim of an originator. We are all familiar with the situation where a paragraph has to be inserted, and because there is not enough room on the page some text has to be carried over to the next page. This also has to be typed again, and the next, and the next, and so on. The insertion of anything more than the odd character missed out during typing almost *always* means a complete retype of the whole page.

Not so with the word processor. Text may be inserted, and the remainder of the page will 'wrap round' and follow on as if the insertion had been there from the beginning. On some systems this is achieved by simply positioning the cursor at the point where the insertion is to begin, and then typing the insertion. The existing text is 'elbowed' along the line to make room for the new, and again 'wraps round' at the end of each line. Other word processors, on the keying of a simple command, will drop the text beyond the insertion point down so as to leave an empty space for the new text. If the insertion continues beyond the end of the line, the remaining text drops again, and continues to do so until the insertion is complete and the command is terminated. Not all the WP software packages are as easy as this. Some require the insertion point to be marked in the text by means of special codes, and the new insertion to be typed elsewhere on the screen. The insertion is only assembled when the text is printed out. Where several insertions are necessary on the same page, editing can become a little more involved. However, it is still quicker and easier than typing the whole page again!

Less checking When any document has to be completely retyped, whether to correct one's own mistakes or as the result of the wishes of an originator, *more* mistakes are likely to occur. This means that both the typist *and* the author have to waste further time checking the entire document. When editing is carried out on a word processor, with subsequent reprinting from the already recorded – and now edited – original, the only parts which need to be rechecked are those where corrections or alterations have been made. The same applies of course when constructing contracts, conveyances and similar documents from 'building-blocks', that is pre-recorded standard paragraphs. The only things which need checking are the variables such as names, addresses and amounts of money peculiar to that particular transaction.

The ease with which corrections, insertions and alterations of all kinds can be made, relieves the typist of a great deal of tension. It is a well-known fact that typists tend to slow down as they progress down a long page of close-packed typescript. The fear of making mistakes, which may mean having to retype the whole page, increases as more and more is committed to paper. On the VDU screen there are no such inhibitions. Mistakes made at the end of a page are corrected as easily as those at the beginning. Nothing at this stage has been printed, so no harm is done. The results are a carefree typist, and an overall increase in production speed.

Because the corrections are all carried out *before* printing-out, there is an end to all those messy corrections to carbon copies. The carbons, where used, are as perfect as the top copy.

The typist as an artist The word processor allows the operator full rein to her creative talents. Alterations to layout, indenting and the creative use of white space, are all much easier when the finished result can be seen on the screen prior to printing-out. Interesting effects are possible using variations of pitch, line-spacing and typeface. With a typewriter a good typist can be a craftswoman – with a word processor she can be an artist!

More job-satisfaction All these factors together result in a considerable increase in job-satisfaction. The ease of operation, the lack of tension, the elimination of all the boring, time-consuming and non-productive repetition, together with the new possibilities for design and layout make the word-processor operator's job a fascinating one. It is significant that wherever word processors have been introduced into an office and the choice between them and typewriters left to the typists, it is always the typewriters that gather dust.

The typist's skill as an investment The operator's skill is a vital factor in the success of a word-processing system. To employ a person who has, or who is capable of attaining this skill is to make an investment far exceeding the value of the hardware concerned. It is unfortunate that there seems to be a false idea in the minds of some employers that the quality of the operator should vary in inverse proportion to the capital cost of the equipment. A manufacturer sponsoring a racing-car for publicity purposes would not dream of entrusting it to a driver from the firm's transport pool. He is quite likely, however, to purchase an expensive word-processor and employ a low-grade typist to operate it on the assumption that the machine will do all the work! It does not seem long since employers were taking copy-typists from the pool, giving them a pound or so extra in their pay-packets, sticking a stethoscope headset in their ears and expecting them to become audio-typists overnight. They soon discovered that the unfortunate girls had in many cases been relying heavily upon their copy for such things as spelling and punctuation, and were totally out of their depth in this new medium. It is inconceivable that a lesson once learned should need to be re-learned in respect of word processing, but regrettably this is so in a minority of cases. It is essential that, in order to extract the maximum use and value from a word processing system, the operators are trained thoroughly *to the extent that the job demands*. This will of course vary from one job to another. The operator who does little more than churn out endless streams of standard letters will not need the proficiency of one who, for example, produces camera-ready copy for the printing of an instruction manual. Returning to audio-typing for the moment, it is now generally accepted that this is the logical medium for input to a word processing system. In realisation of this fact, the emphasis within secretarial courses has shifted from shorthand to audio, and this is now an essential part of every secretarial syllabus.

The word processor operator is too valuable an asset to waste on needless hours of shorthand writing. The word processor will do much to compensate for the inadequacies of the dictator. when the author has used the same word in four successive lines it is easy to substitute 'elegant variations'. Grammatical errors can be ironed out (provided that the operator has the ability to recognise them) and sentences or whole paragraphs transposed where necessary to improve the logical flow. The emphasis, therefore, is not on verbatim note-taking. It is on a good working knowledge of English and a thorough training in proof-reading.

Easily-edited drafts
The ease with which drafts can be produced and subsequently edited should mean that a great deal which would previously have been hand-written can now be dictated onto a machine. From the originator's point of view, it is easier to edit a clear-typed, well-spaced draft than the usual cramped hand-written first efforts. By this means, vast amounts of expensive executive time, formerly occupied by laborious hand-drafting, can be saved.

Value of a trained operator

The true value of the trained operator
The trained operator who knows both the capabilities of the machine *and* the administrative structure and requirements of the job-environment, is often the person most favourably-placed to appreciate the possible uses for word processing within the company. An intelligent merging of the two spheres of knowledge can result in the maximum use of the equipment, and the greatest consequential savings to the company. The factor which will distinguish the *good* operator from the merely proficient, is the way in which the machine is used. The operator must not only know which keys to press in order to achieve certain

results, but must also know how best those results can be used. As with so many things, 'there are more ways of killing a cat . . .' and it is up to the operator in many cases to select the best of a number of possible ways of doing a job.

The word processor operator may at any time be faced with a choice of several different methods. It may, for example, be necessary to move a block of text in order to improve the appearance of a page. It could be moved line by line to its new position; it could be defined as a sentence or paragraph, or even as a rectangular block, or a 'space' above, below or to either side of the text could be inserted, thereby causing it to move to a new position. The choice of method in this simple example would only benefit the *operator* by its speed or convenience. When we come to consider the more complex operations comprising 'information processing' of which the word processor is capable, we will see that it is here that the operator really comes into her own. She is the most favourably-placed to discover new benefits to her employer, in hitherto unthought-of uses for the equipment. The operator's advice will constantly be sought on the best way of doing this or that, or whether such-and-such can be done on the word processor. Conversely, the operator may be able to offer advice on more efficient ways of carrying out prcoedures at present performed by costly or laborious methods.

Print-standard display The good operator will also appreciate the finer points of display, and will use to full advantage the facilities described in the previous section. Layouts of professional 'print-standard' are possible, and the word-processor compositor should be able to produce camera-ready copy for reproduction by offset litho, for such things as auction-sales catalogues or internal house magazines. For externally-circulated house magazines or other high-quality work, a higher standard of reproduction may be required than can be produced by the word-processor printer. In this case it may be possible to communicate directly with a phototypesetter, so that text produced on the word processor can be converted directly into professionally set type, with little or even no intervention by the typesetting house. Considerable savings can thus be made, as it is not now necessary for the text to be re-keyed by the typesetter.

It is not to say that *every* word-processor operator needs to be of an equally high standard of ability. There are many routine jobs which can be done with the aid of word processors which need only a minimum of training over and above the basic skill of typewriting. There will be a need for many different categories of word processor operator, and this need is dealt with more fully in Chapter 7, 'Who will operate it?'

2 Text generation

Four methods

Before the original thought of the executive can be converted by the word processor, it must be presented in some tangible form. This process we will call *Text generation*. Original material – and we are here concerned only with that which has not been previously generated and stored for re-use – can be produced by only four main methods; longhand draft, shorthand notes, a dictation machine, or direct keyboarding, as shown in Figure 3.

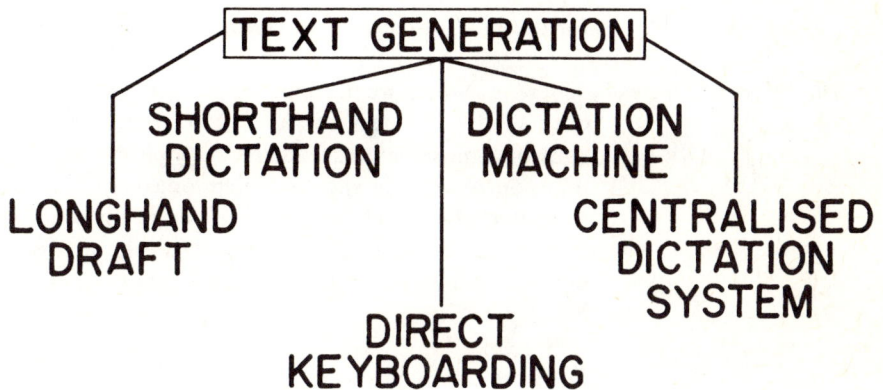

TEXT GENERATION

SHORTHAND DICTATION

DICTATION MACHINE

LONGHAND DRAFT

CENTRALISED DICTATION SYSTEM

DIRECT KEYBOARDING

Fig 3   Word input

Longhand draft   At times, longhand draft can be accepted as the only practicable means of condensing, editing and refining until the precise meaning is conveyed in as few words as possible consistent with the maximum effect. Writers of advertising copy, sales literature or other material, where similar conditions apply, may be excused for using longhand. Important reports, correspondence of a delicate nature, or technical writing, where precision is essential, may also call for a first draft to be produced in longhand. Authors who persist in using longhand for routine correspondence which could well be dictated should be discouraged.

Shorthand notes   Providing a typist with a machine which considerably increases her productivity then compelling her to absent herself from it for long periods to take shorthand dictation makes little sense. Using shorthand as an input to a word processor is rather like buying a fast sports car, fitting it with shafts and harnessing a horse to pull it!

A possible exception to the rule is the 'word-processor secretary' who will compose much of her own input in accordance with brief instructions given by her boss. For the sake of speed, she may well wish to take notes of his instructions in shorthand.

Apart from this perfectly legitimate employment of shorthand as a means of recording brief notes and instructions for her own eventual use, it is likely that even the word-processor secretary will have little need of this time-honoured but obsolescent medium. At first, when the word processor is newly installed and the operator has a box of empty work-disks, there will certainly be a great deal of keying-in of original text. Old habits die hard, and there may be a temptation to continue dictating in the old way. As the work-disks fill up with filed material, much of it re-usable either in its entirety or as 'building blocks' for the construction of standard letters, the need for dictation of complete documents will diminish. At this stage even the most hardened traditionalist will admit the futility of re-dictating long passages which already exist in the files of the word processor. Even when dictation of original text *is* necessary, it makes far more sense to use one of the many forms of dictation machine. This frees the secretary for the kind of *creative* work for which she is undoubtedly fitted.

Dictation machines Where machines are used, by far the greatest proportion of dictation is carried out on individual desk-top units. Modern machines are easy to use, with remote control of most features from the microphone, and refinements such as speed and tone controls, conference and telephone recording, and electronic indexing. The executive who travels, and needs to 'carry his office with him', is catered for by portable units which, like the pocket calculator, are reducing in size. The biggest limiting factor today is the size of the cassette and of the battery needed to drive it.

For note-taking purposes, less elaborate machines are available. These are less sophisticated than the portable dictation machines, but use the same recording media so that they can be used with the desk-based systems. Notes made on these simple machines can be typed from the same transcription machines that are used for office dictation.

It is generally accepted, even among those to whom shorthand is a way of life, that audio is the logical input to a word-processing system. For this reason, wherever word processing is summarily divided into 'input' and 'output', the 'input' designation can usually be taken to refer to a dictation system. In short, dictation machines are *part* of word processing, and as such should be given due consideration when a word processing system is being introduced.

The work of the audio-typist will be considerably enhanced by the use of a word processor. Much routine dictation will be rendered unnecessary by re-use of existing material. In consequence much time will be saved, not only in dictation, but also in the need to check laboriously through entire documents. The 'personal contact', so beloved of the supporters of shorthand, will however become even *more* essential if word processing is to succeed. In order to re-use material which has been previously recorded, the originator must be kept aware of what is available to him. This will entail a close co-operation between the executive and his word-processor secretary. The production of cohesive documents, partly from recorded file-content and partly from additionally dictated text, will necessitate team-work of the highest order. The word-processor secretary will play a great part in saving her boss from the tedium of repetitive dictation.

Direct keyboarding The fourth method of text-generation – direct keyboarding – will perhaps be the slowest of the four to gain momentum, not because it is particularly difficult, but because it does not follow tradition. Comparatively few executives have been trained as keyboard operators. Those who have would probably regard the need to use one as a retrograde step, having once left it behind. The increase in use of personal and small-business computers and other keyboard-based equipment will undoubtedly lead to a wider introduction of teaching keyboarding as a personal skill. Computer terminals will become a common feature in the office, and familiarity with these will also help to overcome any resistance to using a keyboard. Many jobs, particularly those of a creative nature, could be carried out far more easily by direct keyboarding. Instead of the present sequence of 'dictate – wait for draft – edit – wait for finished copy – proof-read – pass for publication', the whole process could be carried out on a word processor in one operation, in a fraction of the time.

3 What is a word processor?

The beginnings

A word processor may be many things to many people. One might as well ask the question, 'What is a typewriter?' or 'What is a photocopier?' There are many levels of typewriter, from the humble portable to the sophisticated electronic proportional-spacing office machine. There are also many grades of photo-copier, from the slow, one-off heat process, semi-domestic machines to the multi-collating, plain-paper copier-duplicators of the huge corporations. One might also ask the question, 'When does a typewriter become a word processor?' because the line of demarcation somewhere around the level of electronic and memory typewriters is very hazy indeed! A manufacturer whose main concern is typewriters, but who introduces, at the top of his range, an electronic machine performing some of the functions of editing and memory, might be tempted to call it a word processor. A similar machine, marketed by a company which also produced powerful word- and data-processing equipment at the top of the range, would to them perhaps only merit the description 'memory typewriter'.

The situation is further complicated by the fact that many electronic typewriters may be upgraded by the addition of disk drives and video displays to perform most of the functions of a low-powered word processor. Indeed, many of these systems are as powerful, or more so, than the word processors of a few years ago.

Word processors in the form of automatic typewriters are not, of course, a new idea. The first one, using a 'pianola roll' of perforated paper, appeared as long ago as 1932. Since then there have been a number of developments using first paper, then magnetic tape or card. The principle was that as the original was typed, a 'master' was produced in recorded form. By feeding this master back into the machine, the original could be reproduced as many times as was required. Magnetic or mechanical coded signals could be introduced to stop the machine at predetermined places to enable the operator to key in variables such as names, addresses, amounts of money and so on. Whole batteries of these were often used for invoicing and credit-control functions, or for sending standard letters containing only a few variables. The speed of operation of these machines was governed by the printing mechanisms then available – conventional type-basket or at best 'golfball' typewriters which could only produce about 15 characters per second (cps). Daisy-wheel printers raised the speed of printing to 45–60 cps. At the time of writing, ink-jet printers are approaching 100 cps with acceptable top-copy quality.

Outside, but bordering on the field of word-processing, ink-jet printers are capable of producing superb multi-colour work, combining a number of basic colours to produce an almost limitless palette of shades and hues. Draft- and line-printers will produce a relatively poor-quality print at extremely high speeds. These are mainly found attached to mainframe computers, or offered as an alternative to letter-quality printers in networked systems. Dual-standard dot-matrix printers are also available which will produce draft-quality printing at a high speed, and work approaching the quality of a daisy-wheel printer at relatively low speeds. The ultimate at the present time (1985) is the laser printer combining laser technology with photocopying techniques to print text and graphics at speeds of from 8 to 30 complete pages per minute.

The microprocessor
The real breakthrough came with the discovery of the microprocessor, or 'the chip' as it has come to be known. The silicon chip is made by taking a wafer of the mineral silicon, and by processes of microphotography, deposition and etching causing it to adopt the characteristics, and perform the functions of, many electronic components. The number of components which it is possible to fashion into one chip numbers many thousands, and increases as new manufacturing techniques are developed.

The first edition of this book stated 'Nothing is possible today which could not have been achieved years ago by large computers'. This may well have been true at that time, and indeed may be so in theory today. In practice however, the capacity and power of the silicon chip and its successors have so far outstripped the early computers that things which are commonplace today could not even have been dreamed of in the early days. Voice synthesis and recognition, for example, use such large quantities of 'memory' that it would have needed computers of leviathan proportions but a few years ago. Now we see these features in pocket-sized games, and programmed learning devices for use by infants! Even in today's terms, what would have required a small battery of silicon chips only a year or two ago is now contained on a single chip. Microprocessors, to give them their proper name, are to be found in practically every field of use, from the cheapest wristwatch sold in every chain store and petrol station to complex equipment capable of diagnosing and repairing its own faults far out in space.

What makes the chip an essential part of word processing is its ability to remember vast amounts of information fed into it in the form of 'digital code'. If it were possible to look into the 'brain' of a computer (or of a word processor, which is a form of computer), all you would see would be millions upon millions of 1s and 0s. This is because the computer can only understand two things, 1 and 0, which it recognises electrically as being 'on' or 'off'. Any number can be expressed as a string of 1s and 0s by using binary notation, as you can see in Figure 4.

	(128)	(64)	(32)	(16)	(8)	(4)	(2)	(1)
1	0	0	0	0	0	0	0	1
2	0	0	0	0	0	0	1	0
3	0	0	0	0	0	0	1	1
4	0	0	0	0	0	1	0	0
5	0	0	0	0	0	1	0	1

Fig 4 Numbers 1 to 5 in binary code

In this, as you will see from the diagram, each column is worth twice that of the one to its right. So instead of the familiar decimal notation of units, tens, hundreds, thousands and so on, we have 1, 2, 4, 8, 16, etc. By adding up the values of the columns containing 1s, we find that we can express any number from 1 (00000001) to 255 (11111111), by a combination of eight digits. Each of these digits in computer terms is called a 'bit' (binary integer), and a group of eight is called a 'byte'. Numbers larger than 255 will of course need to be expressed by more than one byte.

Just as any *number* can be expressed in binary code, it is easy to assign a binary or 'digital' code to the relatively few symbols used in the writing of text. The 'characters', consisting of the upper and lower-case letters, punctuation and other signs, together with the coded 'commands' or instructions to the machine, are each expressed as one byte, consisting of eight bits. The terms 'byte' and 'character' are therefore interchangeable when talking about word processing. You might for example see a word processor described as having 64KB of memory. This would mean that the main memory of the processor would be capable of 'remembering' sixty-four thousand characters and coded instructions. The 'power' or capability of a word processor is largely determined by the size of its memory, though not entirely so. Much depends upon the way in which the memory capacity is used by the program. Some operating systems are more economical in terms of memory use, though possibly at the expense of the operator's convenience. Memory size however is a suitable yardstick for the layman to apply, and in general will give some indication of what kind of features may be expected from a particular machine. So what then *is* the 'memory', and how does it differ from 'storage' – particularly when the two terms are sometimes used indiscriminately?

The human-computer analogy (1)

The easiest way of grasping an unfamiliar subject is by analogy. Let us take the closest possible analogy to a computer – you. You have a brain. When you were forming in the warm comfort of your mother's womb, your brain was being 'programmed' to do many things. It was programmed to cause your heart to beat regularly, pumping the life-giving blood around your body and your lungs to expand and contract from the moment of birth in order to supply that same blood with oxygen. It was programmed to control all the bodily functions which occur without conscious effort such as the digestion of food, and regeneration of damaged tissue. It was also programmed to generate all the 'instinctive' reflexes such as crying from hunger or pain, blinking and swallowing. All of these actions continue in a more or less modified form during your entire lifetime without the need for reinforcement by education.

The computer, or word processor, also has a 'brain', called the main memory. During manufacture, parts of this main memory can be programmed to perform simple or repetitive tasks such as operating the carriage-return at the end of each line, or making sure that incomplete words are transferred to the next line, without conscious effort by the operator.

From the moment you are born (or even before) your brain is being constantly programmed by external stimuli. You learn to walk, talk, and eat in a civilised manner by observing and copying others. You learn to play, partly by imitation, and partly by discovery. From the age where formal education begins, you are taught to express yourself, to read, write, work with figures, and to use existing knowledge in order to acquire more. The 'programming' process continues for the whole of your life. The amount of knowledge and wisdom that you can assimilate is determined by the 'capacity' of your brain.

The ability of the word processor to carry out any of its functions has to be programmed into the main memory either during manufacture, or before use, depending upon which kind of memory it is. It cannot do anything which it has not been programmed to do, and the scope of its ability is governed by the capacity of its main memory.

If you want to use the telephone, you look up the number in the directory, then you retain it in your memory just long enough to dial it. You can then dismiss it from your mind until the next time you want to ring that number.

Small sections of the main memory of a word processor are used for retaining information for a short time only. These are called 'buffer' or 'putaside' memories.

You can do a great deal – walk, talk, play games, cook, ride a bicycle – by reference only to that which is already inside your head. If you want to walk the Pennine Way, or play Bridge, prepare a special meal, or adjust your five-speed gears, you may need to refer to a map, book of rules, recipes or instructions. Because no one is capable of storing in their brain *all* the knowledge that they could ever need, we look to other methods of *storing* information so that it can be recalled only when we need it. By doing this we can infinitely increase our capacity for knowledge, irrespective of the capacity of our own brains to remember things.

A word processor can *store* an infinite amount of text on magnetic cards or disks which can be removed from the machine and kept separately, just like the books in your library. When a particular piece of text is required to be used, that, and only that, is transferred from a disk into the main memory of the word processor. This will consist at the most of a few thousand characters, so the remaining capacity of the main memory can be used to perform tasks requiring many complex operations.

You will understand from this that the *memory* of a word processor is *part of it*, but that *storage* is on disks or cards, which can be removed from the machine and kept separately from it. Such removable storage is known as 'discrete', and the disks or cards are called 'discrete media'. The 'power' of a word processor is measured by the size of its memory. A simple automatic typewriter will have a relatively small memory of only a few thousand characters; the large computer-linked systems may have as many millions. Memories will be described in greater detail later: for the moment let us look at the various arrangements of equipment, or 'configurations', which go to make up what is commonly known as a 'word processor'.

Electronic typewriters   Since the first edition of this book, electronic typewriters have developed to a degree which places them firmly within, albeit at the lower end of, word processing. Indeed, the actual configuration of the component parts – that is the way in which they are assembled – is in many cases the only distinguishing feature. An electronic typewriter commonly comprises a keyboard and printer, usually daisy-wheel, contained within the same casing and resembling in layout the familiar typewriter. Depending upon the power and capabilities of the machine, there may or may not be a panel displaying the last characters to be typed. The machine may have a limited internal memory capable of holding a page or two of text. It will certainly have correction facilities allowing the typist to correct a few pages of text before they are printed out onto paper.

Functions likely to be found on electronic typewriters may include automatic underlining, centring, bold typing, reverse-tone printing and right margin justification. Most electronic typewriters can be linked to other equipment. This makes it possible to add disk drives for increased storage capacity, and screens for text-editing of completed documents. Many of the screen add-on units have additional memory capacity, raising the capabilities of the typewriter to those of a low-powered word processor.

Word processors   Word processors as such, and microcomputers, may be configured in a number of ways: combining keyboard and screen, screen and disk drives or having all three units as separate entities. In most cases the printer is a separate unit. This allows it to be shared between two or more systems, or permits a choice of printer depending upon the quality of output required. There are four main levels of word-processor configuration: stand-alone, shared resource, shared logic and mainframe-based.

Stand-alone systems

This simply means that the system is entirely self-contained. It will stand alone, without the need to be connected to anything other than a mains power socket. It usually consists of four component sections: the Keyboard, the Visual/Video Display Unit (VDU), the Central Processing Unit (CPU) and the Printing Unit.

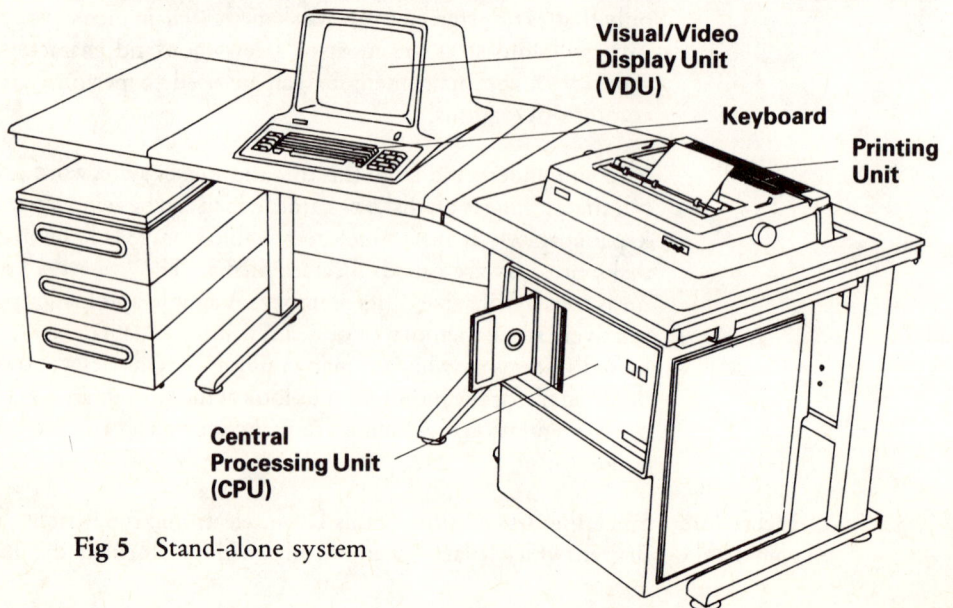

Fig 5   Stand-alone system

The keyboard This is basically the QWERTY keyboard, with a number of additional keys. These 'function' or 'command' keys tell the machine what the operator wishes it to do. The keyboard may be entirely freestanding, and connected by cables to the other components, or it may be built into the same housing as the VDU – or less frequently the printer.

The video display unit (VDU) This is sometimes referred to as a Cathode Ray Tube display (CRT); in other words a television tube.

The most common colours for the display are green characters on a black, or dark grey background, but there is a wide choice of colours from different manufacturers, including black on white, in resemblance to the printed page. There has been much discussion about the colour combination which is likely to be easiest on the eye (in the literal sense). At the time of writing no firm conclusion has been reached, and the choice remains one of personal preference. The question of possible eye-strain caused by continually working from a screen is one which concerns all who are concerned for the welfare of the operators of word processing and computer installations. Again there is at the time of writing no positive proof that working with a VDU can damage the operator's sight. It is generally agreed however that if the operator *already* has some inherent weakness of vision, the VDU may worsen the condition and necessitate corrective measures.

At present there is no satisfactory alternative to the cathode-ray tube for the mass display of information, but developments in opto-electronics, the compound science of optics and electronics, may in time lead to a more acceptable display medium. Already, liquid-crystal displays are beginning to appear on electronic typewriters and portable computers. Alternatively, the cathode-ray tube itself may be improved or treated in some way. Flat television tubes are already in existence, and may soon be commonplace. It could also be argued that the word processor operator does not sit with her eyes glued to the screen any more than the typist looks at the paper upon which she is typing. If working from copy, then *this* is what she will be looking at for most of the time. While audio-typing, her eyes are free to wander, as is usually the case. Only when proof-reading or text-editing is the screen the subject of close scrutiny.

The size, shape and capacity of the VDU screen is infinitely variable at the whim of the manufacturer, each claiming irresistible benefits from his own particular format. At the bottom of the scale we have the 'thin window' single line display which is capable of showing only the last thirty or so characters typed.

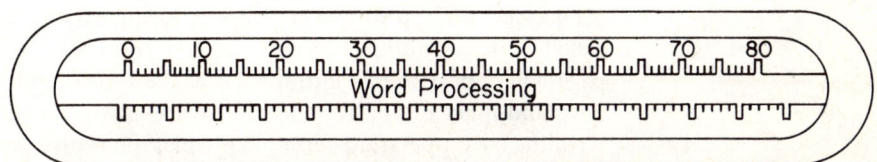

Fig 6 Thin-window display

This enables the operator to correct the instinctively-recognised keying errors which occur with greater or lesser frequency among most typists, but is of little use for text-editing purposes. The thin-window display is found mainly at the bottom of the word-processing range, on machines which are perhaps more correctly classified as electronic typewriters. It is only one step removed from the totally 'blind' systems in which the copy has to be printed out before it can be scanned for errors or required changes. In a blind system a further print-out must then be obtained before it can be seen whether or not any alterations or corrections have been properly carried out. The thin-window does at least allow the operator to see a correction performed within its limited range. The VDU proper, or mass display, is similar in appearance to an ordinary domestic television screen; in the majority of cases it adopts the familiar 'landscape' position where the width is greater than the height. A few manufacturers prefer the upright screen, particularly where a full-page display is offered. The size of the characters and the amount of text that can be viewed at one time vary widely. In a representative selection of models currently available the width of the *display* is standard at 80 characters.

Some of the cheaper microcomputers, particularly those which use an ordinary television screen as a display, are capable of showing only 40 characters. It is unlikely that such equipment will be used for 'serious' word processing, and so may be disregarded in this context.

The actual *page* to be produced can be as wide as 256 characters in some cases. The term 'page' needs explanation. To most typists, and indeed to most laymen, the page is an A4 sheet of paper, or a page in a book. To a word processor, a 'page' is the document which is being produced. This can be any shape or size, up to the capacity of the machine, and the width of paper which the *printer* can hold. There is sometimes confusion between the printed page and the displayed page. The printed page is that which eventually appears as 'hard copy' output by the printer. The *displayed page* is the text on which the operator is currently working, and this can be considerably larger than the screen of the VDU. A displayed page could be as wide as 256 or more characters, or as long perhaps as 94 lines. A screen which would show that number of characters of readable size would need to be about 70cm wide and 40cm high! To overcome this problem, and at the same time to give the typist a display upon which the characters are large enough to be seen easily, the word processor employs a device known as 'scrolling'.

Scrolling The actual *display* is of a certain size, which varies according to the make and type of machine. If the document to be produced is *longer* than the screen permits to be seen all at one time, the page will appear to move upwards as the work progresses, the top of the page disappearing off the top of the screen. This is called 'vertical scrolling'. (See Figure 7.) If the work is *wider* than the display, the page will appear to move to the left as the typist moves along the line, and the left-hand margin will disappear off the edge of the screen. This is 'horizontal scrolling'. By operating certain controls, the typist can move the page up and down, or from side to side in order to look at any part of it. Most word processors and microcomputers are capable of vertical scrolling. Most but not all are capable of *horizontal scrolling*. It may help if you think of the display as a 'window' through which you can view the entire document by instalments, or as the view-finder of a camera, which you move to take in just that part of the scene which you wish to photograph.

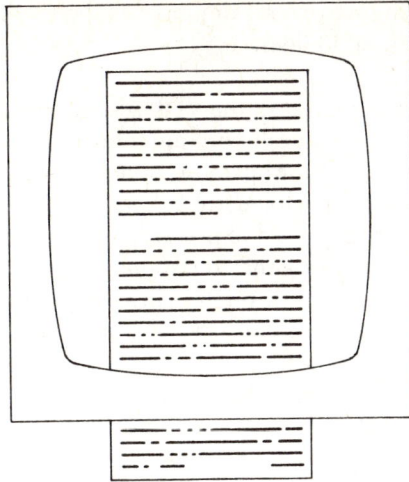

Fig 7   Scrolling

The actual number of lines visible at one time varies from a modest 24 up to as many as 70 – the latter evidently on an upright screen. The number of lines on the displayed page can exceed 90. Scrolling is an automatic function. If you are typing across a wide document, the page will move to the left as you type. Similarly, when you come to the bottom of the screen, the page automatically moves upwards, you don't just run out of screen! VDUs are usually described as being half-page or full-page displays, relating to the amount of an ordinary A4 page which would be visible. A screen showing around 20–30 lines would therefore be rated as a half-page, and the 50–70 line display would be full-page. You should bear in mind that the greater the number of lines and characters displayed, the smaller they must be, as the size of the screen does not vary greatly. A full-page display of small characters may be more tiring to the operator than would a half-page of characters twice the size. This is particularly important in a teaching or training situation where groups of students need to see the screen while the operations are described to them. Some manufacturers offer alternative formats on the same screen – half-page large characters for normal working, and an alternative full-page display for text-editing and layout adjustment. One maker in fact offers no fewer than three possibilities: 32 lines × 128 characters; 32 × 256; and 70 × 102. In advertisements and sales literature you may see a VDU specified as '28 × 80 scrolling to 94 × 250'. The smaller figure is the number of lines, the larger the number of characters per line in each case. The machine thus described would have a display of 28 lines of 80 characters (half-page), but the actual document produced could be as large as 94 lines long or 250 characters wide.

The size of the displayed page is governed by the amount of main memory which has been set aside for that purpose. It will therefore consist of a finite number of characters – say 8000 as an example. It follows therefore that as the page width setting is *increased*, the number of lines possible becomes fewer. Taking the common provision of 80 characters wide by 94 lines long, the number of *characters* allowed would be 80 × 94 = 7520. (Remember that the page description and format lines will also take up space in the memory). If you increase the line length to the maximum of 256, you will find that this allows you to display only about 30 lines.

Status information As well as the text being typed, the VDU also displays what is known as 'status information'. This will be dealt with more fully in a later chapter, but briefly it consists of information to the operator. It includes such things as page width and length, margin and tabulator settings, and any special function which the machine has been programmed to perform. On more advanced systems, a series of 'prompts' consisting of either questions or instructions will appear on the screen to guide the operator through an involved 'command sequence'. This will be dealt with in the chapter entitled 'How does it do it?'

Cursor A cursor indicates to the operator where she is actually working on the screen. This takes the form of a flashing signal, an underscore or half-tone effect, which tells the operator the position of the next character to be typed. This is used to locate corrections, insertions and deletions, or to define the limits of a block of type which is to be the subject of some further operation. To enable the operator to locate the cursor quickly, its horizontal position is usually duplicated at the top of the screen. The position of the cursor may also be indicated numerically in the status lines.

Brightness A brightness control is usually provided to allow for individual preference on the part of the operator, or differing conditions of ambient light, that is the level of light in the room at the time.

The central processing unit (CPU) This is the 'brain' of the word processor. It is the computer which controls all the functions of the system and determines the capabilities or 'power' of a particular configuration. In the stand-alone system the CPU is a self-contained unit, exclusive to a particular word-processor and to an individual operator. Anything stored within the memory of that CPU is available only to its own operator and cannot be 'accessed' or made use of by any other operator or machine. This makes 'stand-alone' a very secure system.

Main memory The CPU contains the main memory of the system, which holds the material, or 'page', which is being currently worked on, and all the 'program', or instructions, which enable the processor to carry out the various functions of which it is capable. The program, if it is not permanently built into the machine, is usually recorded on a disk. The text to be worked on is *also* recorded on disks. This often leads to confusion between program disks, and 'working disks'. Let us try to resolve this as it is one of the basic concepts which are needed to help you to understand how a system works.

Volatile memory All the more powerful processors have what is called a 'volatile' memory. A volatile substance is one which evaporates easily, such as petrol, methylated spirit, or dry-cleaning fluid. If you leave a shallow dish containing one of these in a warm room overnight, it will be empty by morning; the contents will have evaporated into the air. In just the same way, the contents of a volatile memory disappear as soon as the machine is switched off. Before you can use the processor again, it must be reprogrammed. This allows you to use the *same* memory for many different kinds of job. Today, for example, you may need to do some straightforward typing of business letters, or a long report. Tomorrow, you may need to extract certain information from your personnel files which are kept on disks. The next day you may be back to ordinary typing, or you may wish to use a 'graphics' program, if you have one, to rule up a new form, or draw an organisation chart. The day after, you could find yourself using the 'arithmetic' program to update a price-list by 10 per cent, or to issue some invoices. To have the ability *permanently* to do all these things would mean that the word processor would need a main memory of significant size, probably 128K or more of which only a small part would be in use at any one time. The same effect can be achieved by using a volatile memory, and programming it separately for each different *kind* of job. Even this can become tedious in a full-scale word-processing operation, so the tendency of the more powerful machines is to have several programs recorded on one disk. These are loaded into the main memory of the machine, and it is then possible to skip from one kind of operation to another without reprogramming the system.

Programming On all but the most elementary systems such as electronic typewriters, where the program is built into one or more microprocessors during manufacture, the word processor has to be programmed before use. The program is in most cases provided by the manufacturer of the equipment, or the software supplier, already recorded on a disk. At the start of the day, or of a particular type of job, a program disk appropriate to the task is inserted into one of the disk drives in the central processing unit, shown in Figure 8.

Fig 8 Inserting a disk into a disk drive

The door of the disk drive is closed and the disk then spins very fast. All the information and instructions which have been recorded on the disk by the manufacturer are transferred into the main memory of the machine. After a short time, usually only a matter of seconds, an audible or visible signal indicates to the operator that programming is complete. At this point, the status information appears at the top of the screen. The programme disk can now, in most cases, be removed. The machine is in the same state of readiness as a simpler machine with a permanently built-in programme as soon as it is switched on. It is ready to begin work. On some word processors the programme disk has to be left in the machine during operation. In this case, only one of the two disk drives is available for the insertion of a 'work disk'. On others, the 'system disk' which carries the program can also be used for storing files of text.

The work disk If you have a system which uses separate disks for programming and for storing text, you will now insert a 'work disk'. This is a disk which *you* create, from one of a number of blank disks supplied with, or in addition to, the equipment. Every time that you produce new text, either from dictation or other means of input, you record the completed version on a floppy disk. You can recall the text to the VDU screen at any time, or you can ask the printing unit to print from a disk while you use the screen for something else. As you record, or 'file' each item, you give it a name, or a reference, or both. An index is automatically created on the disk, and you can call this to the screen, thus seeing exactly what is filed on that particular disk. By keying-in the name and reference you can then call to the screen any of the documents – or 'pages' – which are filed on that disk.

It should be stated here that some word processors are what is known as 'document-oriented' and some are 'page-oriented'. This refers to the way in which text is stored on the disk and of course to how it may be recalled to the screen. In a *document-oriented* system, a complete document, consisting of however many pages, may be stored under a file- or text-name. When it is required to recall the document to the screen, the *whole* document is displayed from the beginning. It is then necessary to scroll through the text until the required page is reached. In a *page-oriented* system, each page may be stored separately, each with its own page number and possibly an additional reference indicating the contents; but under a common text-name. It is thus possible to call to the screen only the page on which the operator wishes to work, without needing to scroll through the entire document in order to find it.

The type of 'orientation' also affects the method by which editing takes place. On a document-oriented system, text-editing is often 'destructive'. This means that as you alter text on the screen, the text on the disk is also changed without reference to the operator, and the original version is thereby destroyed. On a page-oriented system, the operator has a choice of whether to destroy or retain the original version. Having brought a page to the screen, you can then edit or adapt it in any way you choose. When you have finished whatever you are doing with that page, you have the choice of 'updating' the original, in which case its place on the disk is taken by the revised version, or leaving the original one where it is. You can then invent a new text-name, and file the edited version *as well* as the original.

If your word processor has two disk-drives, it may be possible to 'merge' information filed on two work disks. For example, you can merge a standard letter on one disk with a mailing list of names and addresses recorded on another. This is of course only possible if both disk drives are available for work disks.

Remember that some systems require the program disk to be left in one drive, thus leaving only one free for work disks.

To reinforce the difference between a program disk and a work disk, let us return to our 'human-computer' analogy. This time however, we will use your doctor as the example.

The human-computer analogy (2)

Imagine that you are visiting the doctor complaining of a sore throat, and that in a few days time you have to give an important speech, or sing in a concert. Your doctor is a very powerful 'information-processor', with a brain, or 'main memory' of large capacity. His initial 'programming' took place during at least five years' training in medical school and hospital, and he is constantly being updated in the light of his day-to-day experience. He *could* no doubt, if he wished, use the power of his 'main memory' to remember the names, addresses, and medical histories of his patients, together with the names, properties and side-effects of every known drug. If he did so, however, it is likely that he could have little energy left for diagnosing ills, and prescribing cures.

What he does in practice is to use 'discrete media' for storing information, thus leaving the power of his brain available for the work which is of greater importance. As you enter his surgery, he is likely to be looking at a card which his receptionist has given to him prior to your arrival. This is your Medical Record Card, and is the 'working disk' from which the doctor is now transferring information about you to the 'VDU' of his conscious thought. When he has done so, he will then ask questions, or observe symptoms, which will enable him to 'edit' or 'update' the information which he has so far. By mentally 'keying-in' this new knowledge, he can 'merge' it with that which is already available to him from your record card. He sees, for example, that you have a previous record of tonsillitis, and that previously certain drugs have been successful in effecting a cure. From his observations and questions, he establishes that you have a recurrence of the complaint. This time, however, greater speed is necessary to ensure your fitness for the impending concert. He may now decide to employ a second 'working disk' in the form of the *Pharmacopoeia* which he takes down from his shelf to look up the name and properties of a new drug. Having 'merged' this new information with that already in his 'main memory', he now 'prints out' the results in the form of a prescription and advice. As you murmur your thanks and rise to leave, the doctor takes up the next patient's Medical Record Card, and begins to repeat the process.

Memories are made of this

It is desirable at this stage that you should know something about the different types of *memory* which you will come across in descriptions of word processors and similar micro-processor-based equipment. Memories come in three main kinds: ROM, PROM and RAM. If you are as mystified as I was when I first encountered these acronyms let me explain that they stand for Read Only Memory, Programmable Read Only Memory, and Random Access Memory. At the moment these are mainly composed of one or more microprocessors, though it appears that before long the silicon chip may be superseded.

Read Only Memory (ROM)

This is the kind of memory chip that you might find in your television game, or pocket calculator, or controlling your washing-machine or video-recorder. It is the simplest kind of memory, used when only a limited number of functions need to be remembered, or few alternatives considered. The functions, or responses to alternative stimuli, are programmed into the memory during its manufacture and cannot be changed. They are sometimes referred to as being 'burned-in' though this is a far from accurate description. 'Built-in' would perhaps be more apt.

ROM in word processing is used in electronic typewriters, in relatively simple word processors, and to control some of the basic and often-used functions in the more advanced word-processing equipment. It is the kind of memory which forms the part of the 'brain' of the word processor which is permanently programmed to perform the simple repetitive tasks – the 'bodily functions' referred to in our 'human-computer' analogy. This leaves the powerful volatile memory free for the more complex operations possible on a disk-based machine. In some word processors, the entire main memory is ROM. This means that it will only ever do what it was programmed to do when it was built. It cannot be reprogrammed to perform a variety of functions; nor can it be updated by using more advanced programs.

Programmable Read Only Memory (PROM) This is a tricky one. It is programmable, but only by the manufacturer or service engineer. The memory is built in such a form that it can be used for many different applications, from working the cash till in your local supermarket to controlling the traffic-lights in the street outside. It is supplied to the equipment manufacturer, who programmes it to suit his own particular needs. As far as the user is concerned, it is still only ROM, but if for any reason the manufacturer wishes to change the function or sequence of operations of whatever it is that he is making, he can erase the program, perhaps by exposing the chip to ultra-violet light, and reprogram it to suit his changed requirements.

Random Access Memory (RAM) This is a completely different kettle of fish! It is more versatile, totally different in concept, and the heart of most word processors. The fundamental difference between ROM and RAM is that with ROM the memory remains all the time, even when the machine is switched off. With RAM, *the memory is programmed by the user* each time the machine is required for use. At first this might appear to be something of a nuisance, but when you consider the implications, you will quickly realise the benefit to the user. In the first place, programming the machine is not a complicated keyboard operation, but is carried out by simply inserting a special program-disk or cassette, and allowing it to run for a certain length of time. This time varies with the medium used. A disk will programme a machine in a matter of seconds; a cassette will take rather longer, depending upon the type used. In any case the operation is only likely to take a minute or two at most.

At the present state of the art, using silicon chip RAM, the program disappears as soon as the machine is switched off. The memory empties, and must be reprogrammed before the machine will function again. Developments in more advanced kinds of memories, including the 'bubble' memory and others even more futuristic, suggest that it may be practicable to combine the advantages of ROM and RAM, so that a program is retained for a certain length of time even after the machine is switched off. This would avoid the necessity to reprogram after accidental disconnection, or a power cut, or even after a short break.

Advantages of RAM   The main advantages of RAM in terms of machine selection is that it is the program, not the hardware, which determines what the machine can do. A word processor using RAM will not in itself go out of date, as it can be up-dated by the use of more advanced software – which is another name for the program. Such systems are often described as being 'software based'.

As far as the main memory is concerned, you will now be better-placed to understand the technical specifications of a word processor. If, for example, it should be described as having 8K of ROM, or 64K of RAM, this will be an indication to you, not only of the capacity, but also of the power in terms of the kind of functions which it can perform. You can then use this as a means of comparison between different models of machine. It may help you to remember the three types of memory if you liken them to the menu board in the works canteen or college refectory (see Figure 9). The word 'MENU' at the top is carved or cast into the material of which the board is made and cannot in any way be altered without destroying the board: This is ROM (Read Only Memory).

Down the side of the board are painted the words 'Starters', 'Main Course', 'Sweets' and 'Drinks'. If you called in a signwriter (manufacturer), he could remove these words by scraping them off, or using chemicals, and replace them with 'Lunch' and 'Tea'. This is PROM (Programmable Read Only Memory).

The remainder is a blackboard upon which the cooks chalk the day's fare every morning, rubbing out each evening when they clean down the counter. This is RAM (Random Access Memory).

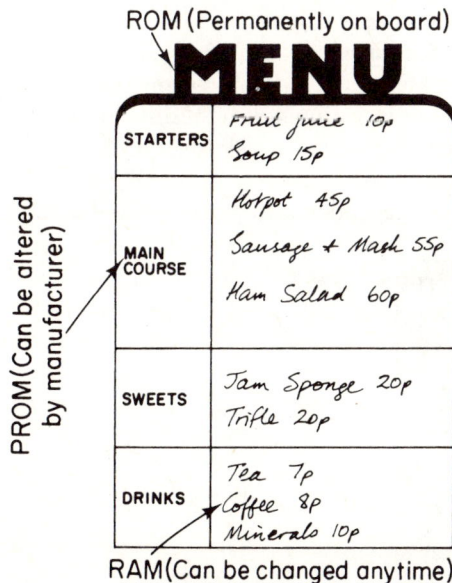

ROM (Permanently on board)

MENU

STARTERS	Fruit juice 10p Soup 15p
MAIN COURSE	Hotpot 45p Sausage + Mash 55p Ham Salad 60p
SWEETS	Jam Sponge 20p Trifle 20p
DRINKS	Tea 7p Coffee 8p Minerals 10p

PROM(Can be altered by manufacturer)

RAM(Can be changed anytime)

Fig 9   ROM, PROM and RAM

Text storage   Further storage, as opposed to memory, is usually quoted as being so many characters – or more meaningfully, so many A4 pages – on disk, floppy disk, cartridge, etc. This means that the storage capacity on discrete media, being separate from the machine itself, is infinitely expandable by the addition of further disks, cartridges, etc. This off-machine storage is achieved by the use of a selection of media according to the preference of the manufacturer.

The first such medium was the 'pianola roll' of the first crude automatic typewriter back in 1932. This was soon replaced by paper tape or punched cards in which holes in the tape or card represented different characters according to their position. Punched paper tape is still used in many applications, including sending Telex messages, and in photo-typesetting. Many word-processor manufacturers in the past have offered paper-tape punches as optional extras, so that the word processor can be used in conjunction with a telex machine or phototypesetter. In most cases this is no longer necessary, as the various types of equipment can communicate electronically.

Most word processors now use magnetic media in a variety of forms. Before we go on to look at these, we must first get to know some of the terms used in describing them and measuring their capacity for storage.

Bits and bytes You will remember that in Chapter 1 it was explained that all information fed into a computer must be reduced to strings of 1s and 0s. These individual 1s and 0s are known in computer terminology as 'bits'. The bits are assembled in groups of (usually) eight to represent numbers, or characters of text, and these groups are then called 'bytes'. In word-processing the terms 'character' and 'byte' are used indiscriminately to describe the capacity of a memory or store. Byte is often abbreviated to capital 'B' and is shown together with K for Kilo – a thousand – or M for Mega – a million. The description 5KB applied to a magnetic card simply means that it will store five thousand characters of text. This approximates to one A4 page, and often capacities are quoted as so many pages rather than characters. This unit of measurement is more meaningful to the typist or office manager when assessing needs. Let us look at the different kinds of magnetic media. These are of three main types: card, disk (or disc) and tape.

Magnetic card This was the first magnetic medium to be linked with a golf-ball typewriter, thus

Fig 10   Magnetic card

producing the beginning of word processing as we know it today. As you read in the previous section, a magnetic card usually holds 5 000 characters – one A4 page. There are however, magnetic cards advertised as holding 8 000 or even 10 000 characters according to the make of the machine. Because of its relatively small capacity, the magnetic card (shown in Figure 10) is to be found towards the bottom of the product range, being suitable only for fairly basic kinds of operation. For the same reason, it is usually associated with the ROM (Read Only Memory) type of processor of fairly low power and few functions.

Tape cassettes   Tape cassettes (shown in Figure 11) are also usually found in low-powered systems, editing typewriters and some of the early 'blind' word processors without VDU screens. The main disadvantage of a tape cassette for this kind of work is the amount of time necessary to 'access' or find a particular spot on the tape. To do this, the tape must be wound from one spool to the other – an operation which may take seconds, or tens of seconds. As a comparison, information can be called up from a disk in an average time of 260 *milliseconds*, which is around the speed of light. The capacity of a tape cassette is usually between 50K and 250K, though one manufacturer boasts 4.3 *Megabytes* – 4.3 million characters – on a special four-track tape.

Although the tape cassette earns low honours as a means of primary storage for the reasons given, it really comes into its own as a back-up medium. Some of the more powerful word-processing systems and many of the bigger micro- and mini-computers use hard disks to store text and data instead of magnetic cards or floppy disks. These carry vast quantities of information, consequently the risk of losing data through accident or malfunction is proportionately higher. To minimise this risk, operators of these systems employ a regular backup routine whereby the contents of the hard disk are copied onto another medium at short regular intervals. If for some reason the disk should become 'corrupted' or spoiled, all that will be lost will be what has been produced since the most recent backup. All the data up to that point can then be re-copied back to the hard disk, and the comparatively small losses made good. As the question of speedy access does not arise, the tape cassette is an ideal and cheap backup medium. Some backup mechanisms consist of high-speed drives called 'tape streamers' with specially constructed cassettes. Others use standard cassettes, which are simply 'posted' into slots in the central processor in much the same way as into a car cassette player.

Fig 11   Tape cassette

Most word processors use one or other of the various types of disk. There are two broad types; rigid, and flexible, usually called 'floppy'.

Rigid disks   The rigid, or hard disk is mostly used on large computers, and in word processing systems where the central processor is shared by a number of operators. The storage capacity of the rigid disk is so large that it is quoted in MB – megabytes. Figures of capacity current at the time of writing range from 1.25 MB to 80.4 MB on a single disk. Several disks can be used together, giving in excess of 320 MB, that is 320 million characters available for use at one time. If we take the 5000 characters of the magnetic card as representing one A4 page, 320 MB gives us access to 64000 pages of text. Hard disks are sometimes enclosed in a special casing for easy handling and transport called a disk cartridge. (See Figure 12.) One of these can hold between 10 MB and 80 MB – 2000 to 16 000 pages.

Winchester disks   A hybrid, midway between the rigid disk and the floppy, is known as a Winchester disk pack. In this, a number of thin disks are permanently sealed into a container which also holds the drive mechanism. As the disks are thus isolated from the atmosphere, the Winchester can be used in a normal office environment, without the precautions attached to most hard-disk installations. As the disks inside a Winchester are the same size as floppy disks, it is possible to construct the unit to occupy no more space than would a standard floppy-disk drive. It is therefore sometimes feasible to replace a normal disk drive with a Winchester, vastly increasing the storage capacity of a system without adding to its material bulk.

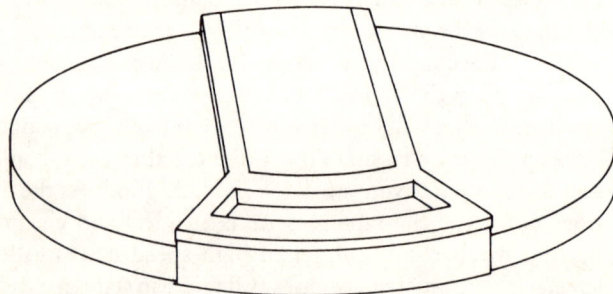

Fig 12   A disk cartridge

Floppy disks   The terms floppy disk, flexible disk, and diskette are generally interchangeable. They all refer to a disk of flexible plastic, 8″ in diameter, looking rather like a '45' gramophone record in its sleeve. It is sealed into the sleeve and never removed from it. The whole thing is inserted into the slot in the central processor when required for use. Floppy disks can be single- or double-sided, and hold on average around 300 KB, though I have seen it stated that 1.6 million characters can be stored on a floppy disk.

The capacity of a floppy disk in terms of text will obviously vary from one make of machine to another. An average floppy disk used on a word processor will hold, in theory, around 128 A4 pages. In practice, because the text-names themselves take up disk space, it is likely that around 100 A4 pages will be stored before the disk is full. Some disks will hold considerably more than this, depending upon how they are made and 'configured' to store the text. Figure 13 shows what a floppy disk looks like.

The mechanism which spins the disk inside the processor, scans it and either 'reads' information from it to the VDU screen or main memory of the machine, or 'writes' on to it from the screen, is called the 'disk drive'. There may be two or more disk drives in a CPU, thereby enlarging the storage capacity, or enabling material from different disks to be merged into a single document by inserting two work disks and working from both simultaneously.

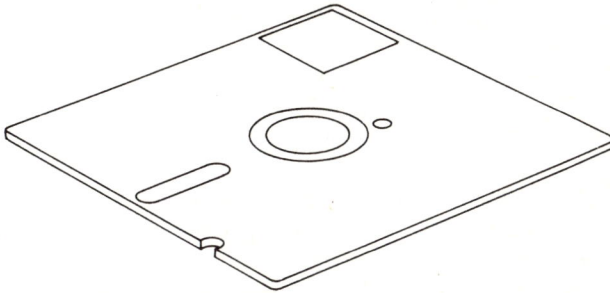

Fig 13 Floppy disk

Mini-floppy disks   The mini-floppy disk, or mini-diskette, is similar in principle and appearance to its bigger brother, but is only 5¼″ in diameter, but in spite of its smaller size may hold as much as or more than an 8″ disk. The development of double-density, double-sided disks has made possible the increased storage capacity in a smaller space. At the time of writing, one manufacturer has announced a 5¼″ mini-floppy disk holding 1.6 *Mega*bytes of data. By the time you read this, even that figure may have been surpassed.

Micro-floppy disk   These have appeared in both 3″ and 3½″ sizes and contrary to expectation – again at the time of writing – hold an amazing *megabyte* of data. From this it will be seen that the capacity of a disk to store data can increase in inverse proportion to its physical size.

Magnetic media in general are continually the subject of further research and, like the microprocessor, from time to time achieve 'quantum leaps'. New methods of manufacture involving electroplating special oxides onto ultra-thin disks already promise capacities far greater than are achievable at present and may indeed be commonplace by the time these words appear in print.

Diode laser disk   The rainbow-hued silver of the diode laser optical disk is now familiar in the domestic field as a means of video recording. The disk consists of a thin layer of a special alloy sandwiched between layers of glass. The data is recorded in the form of minute pits burned into the surface of the alloy by a laser beam. Typically, a single diode laser disk will hold around 500 000 pages of A4, though again different manufacturers have used differing techniques and standards. A variation of the diode laser is the 'Megadoc' system in which a number of disks are selected mechanically in much the same way as the records in an old-fashioned juke box.

Summary   To sum up, the central processing unit is a computer. It has its own main memory, which is supplemented by information fed into it from storage media such as magnetic cards, tapes or disks. It can be ROM-based, which means that its capabilities are limited by the program which exists permanently in its memory. It can be RAM, or software-based, which means that its capabilities are decided by the program which is fed into it each time it is used. It can be exclusive to one operator in a stand-alone system, or, as we shall shortly see, it can be shared by a number of operators. It can use magnetic cards, tapes, or disks of various kinds. It can perform functions from the basic insertions and corrections of the simplest electronic typewriter, to the complex text-editing operations which you will read about in the next chapter, 'What will it do?' First let us look at the piece of equipment which completes the basic configuration of the stand-alone system – the printing unit.

The printer   The printer is the part of the word processor which actually produces the 'hard copy', or 'finished document', in a form in which it can be removed from the machine and handled, transmitted and stored, or read and acted upon by a recipient. This is the 'conversion back' from machine language, that is, digital code, into a form which can be assimilated by human beings.

The earliest automatic typewriters, and many derivatives which were still in use until comparatively recently, used ordinary type-bar mechanisms in which the type was arranged in the familiar semi-circular 'basket'. Even electrically-operated versions of this were painfully slow, and a notable improvement was effected by the invention of the 'golf ball' single-element typewriter. In this the type-head, in the form of a truncated sphere, moves along a fixed platen. This raised the printing speed to fifteen characters per second (15cps) and this same golf-ball typewriter is still used as the printer for some of the lower-priced systems.

Dot-matrix heads   For many years now, computers have been able to print-out at great speeds using dot-matrix printers. In these, the characters are formed by a number of dots (see Figure 14).

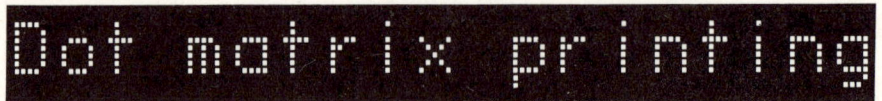

Fig 14   Dot-matrix printing

These are produced by the impact upon a ribbon of a number of wires or needles contained in a rectangular printhead and actuated by electromagnets. The 'resolution' or formation of the characters depends upon two factors: (i) the number of needles in the matrix, and (ii) the number of 'passes' taken to produce the characters. The sample shown was produced on a matrix of 7×5, as you will see if you count the dots in the vertical and horizontal lines in the letter 'D'. A matrix containing a greater number of smaller needles will be capable of producing more complex shapes, and approaching more nearly the proper formation of the letters. High-resolution matrix printers can also print graphics, logotypes, and offer a choice of fonts for normal text. Some are also capable of producing letter-quality work which almost equals that of a daisy-wheel. This is achieved by multi-pass techniques in which the head first prints the basic form of the character, then offsets slightly from its original position and prints the same line again. The new dots produced by the second pass fill the spaces between those of the first pass and the 'dotty' effect is to a great extent dispelled. This of course slows down the speed of printing but even so this is likely to be faster than the average daisy-wheel printer.

The daisy-wheel printer The most widely-accepted solution is the adoption of the 'daisy-wheel' printer. The printing element, as the name implies, consists of a wheel with flexible arms radiating from the centre like the petals of a daisy as shown in Figure 15. The type-heads are to be found at the tips of the petals. Most carry a single character at the tip of each 'petal' but some printers have two characters on each and use a

Fig 15   Daisy-wheel

shift mechanism. This doubles the number of characters possible on a single daisy-wheel from the normal 96 to a possible 192 – though this number is rarely required. The printing element moves along a fixed platen, which is usually long enough to accept A3 paper. Special wide-track printers are also available for applications using large paper-sizes. Dual-head daisy-wheel printers have two printheads, each of which can carry a different type font. This makes possible the printing of mathematical formulae using Greek and special mathematical symbols. Alternatively the dual-head printer can be used for dual-font work in which, for example, italics alternate with ordinary print. For all these applications, special software is required to drive the printer. If the Greek/maths feature is required, it may also be necessary to modify the VDU in order to display the special characters on the screen.

Some daisy-wheel printers are bi-directional; that is to say they print both ways, left to right and right to left. Because what is to be printed already exists in its complete form stored on a work-disk or held in the memory, the machine does not have to type in sequence as a human operator would have to. Hence it does not need to waste time carriage-returning at the end of each line. It simply linespaces and prints every alternate line backwards, from right to left. There are at present several speeds of daisy-wheel printer available, the most common being 45 characters per second, and 55 characters per second. To gain some idea of what this sounds like, listen to the 'mains hum' produced by a faulty fluorescent light fitting, or a record player or tape recorder. In the UK, mains frequency is 50 Hertz, or 50 cycles per second, which is not far off the 45 or 55 *characters* or key-strokes, of the printer. Mains hum then, approximates in *speed* to the sound of a daisy-wheel printer in action. Translated into the language of the typist, assuming the British standard of five characters to the word, the machine is typing at 540 wpm!

A word of warning – in the United States, a word is sometimes taken to consists of *six* characters to our *five*. In sales-literature from an American-based manufacturer you may therefore see a daisy-wheel printer rated at 450 wpm, and in another leaflet what appears to be an identical printer producing 540 wpm. Don't be fooled – it's the same printer. The important thing is the characters per second (cps) and this will be seen to be the same in both cases.

The daisy-wheel type-head is easily changed, and a great many different type-styles are available, including special ones for foreign languages and mathematical symbols. Printwheels are manufactured to print in 10, 12, 15 and 20 pitch, and for proportional spacing. If the word processor has a 'graphics' facility to print vertical lines, it is necessary to ensure that the printwheel chosen has the required character for this purpose.

Thimble printers A variation of the daisy-wheel has the printing element formed like a cup or thimble, as if the daisy was half-closed.

Continuous stationery In many applications of word processing it is necessary to use continuous-feed stationery. For this purpose, it is possible to fit what is called a 'tractor-feed' mechanism to the printer. This consists of sprockets, or toothed wheels, geared to the platen roller and set to the width of stationery to be used. The letter-heads, forms, envelopes, or whatever is to be typed, are attached by the top edge to a continuous backing-sheet, folded concertina fashion, and having holes down each side which locate with the sprocket wheels of the drive. When the work is completed, the letter-heads, etc, are cleanly separated from the backing sheet, and are then indistinguishable from individually-typed top copies. Another form of continuous stationery has the paper cut almost through, so that when printing is completed the edges containing the sprocket-holes can be cleanly removed. This saves the expense of a backing sheet, and the result is barely distinguishable from a normal A4 sheet of paper.

Wide-bed models of the daisy-wheel printer (up to 26″) are available for specialised applications. These have an extra-long platen, and will accept wide forms, ledger-sheets and so on.

The use of this method of printing introduces the possibility of an unusual 'reverse-tone' effect found on certain electronic typewriters. In this the print-head types a continuous block of unrelieved black. It then uses a correcting ribbon to *remove* ink in the form of the character. This then shows white against a black background.

reverse-tone

Fig 16   Reverse-tone printing

Ink-jet printers   Printing at speeds up to twice those of the daisy-wheel, and producing work of comparable quality, the ink-jet printer is favoured by a number of word-processor manufacturers and even more computer manufacturers. The characters are produced by the deposition of tiny drops of very quick-drying ink onto the paper. As the principle is similar to that of the dot-matrix printer, the ink-jet is neither bounded by limitations of typestyle, nor the availability of characters on a printwheel. It also has the advantage of being almost silent in operation, unlike the impact printers. The ink-jet printer can produce its tiny dots anywhere on the page, and can therefore tackle graphics, logotypes or characters of any shape or design. Some ink-jet printers are capable of colour work, and can produce an almost limitless variety of shades and hues from a selection of basic colours contained in easily-changed cassettes.

Being a non-impact process, the ink-jet of course cannot cut stencils.

Image printers   The image printer (see Figure 17) represents a point at which a number of office-machine technologies combine to produce an extremely versatile piece of equipment. In some, low-powered laser beams scan the page, producing print and graphics with extremely high resolution – many thousands of dots per square inch. As with the ink-jet and dot-matrix printers, it is immaterial to the laser beam whether it is producing text or graphical material. Some hundreds of different type fonts can be produced, and the operator is able to design graphics from the keyboard. Two types of laser are in current use: the gas laser and the semi-conductor laser. The latter is claimed to be safer and to last longer.

The other method of image printing uses ion deposition which, using a matrix of electrodes, charges a drum with fine dots in the pattern of the image to be produced. Paper and toner are pressed together between the charged drum and a high-pressure roller, and particles of toner adhere to the charged dots, thus producing the image.

Both these methods print hard copy directly from digital signals produced by microprocessor-based equipment. The source may be a word processor or computer producing text or graphics from the keyboard, or it may be some other form of input device reading or scanning existing images in hard-copy form. Distance is no object. The image scanner can be contained within the same cabinet as the printer – which then becomes a photocopier; or it may be separated by yards, miles or continents – in which case it becomes a facsimile copier. It should be seen from this that the image copier, though expensive at first sight, may well be economic in that it can replace several other devices. The same equipment may function as a printer, photocopier, optical character reader, facsimile copier and message-receiver. It is almost totally silent in operation and extremely fast, printing whole pages in seconds.

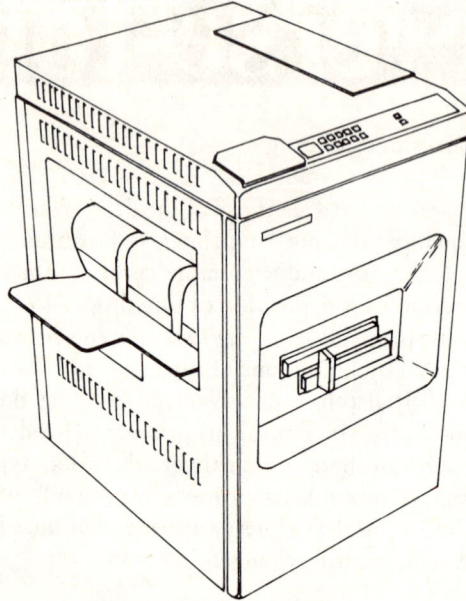

Fig 17 Image printer

Shared-logic and mainframe systems

Up to now in our description of the various component parts of the system, we have assumed in most cases that the end result will be a stand-alone word processor. A stand-alone system is self-contained, with one keyboard, one VDU, one CPU, and probably, but not necessarily, the exclusive use of a printer. There is nothing to say, however, that this will always be the case. In large applications, where the size of the operation justifies the high capital cost of the initial installation, a shared-logic system as shown in Figure 18 may be practicable.

In this kind of system, a large, powerful central processor using hard disk, or Winchester disk pack is shared by a number of operators, each with her own terminal. The terminal consists simply of a keyboard and VDU, which allows the individual operator to access and work with the enormous store of information in the common CPU. Printers are also a shared facility, and it is not unusual in these cases to find a choice of printer to match different needs. There may be daisy-wheel printers for normal top-copy work, and a dot-matrix printer working at something like 2000 wpm for preliminary drafts. It is also likely that there will be interfacing, that is the ability to work with Telex or phototypesetters, either directly or through the medium of punched paper tape.

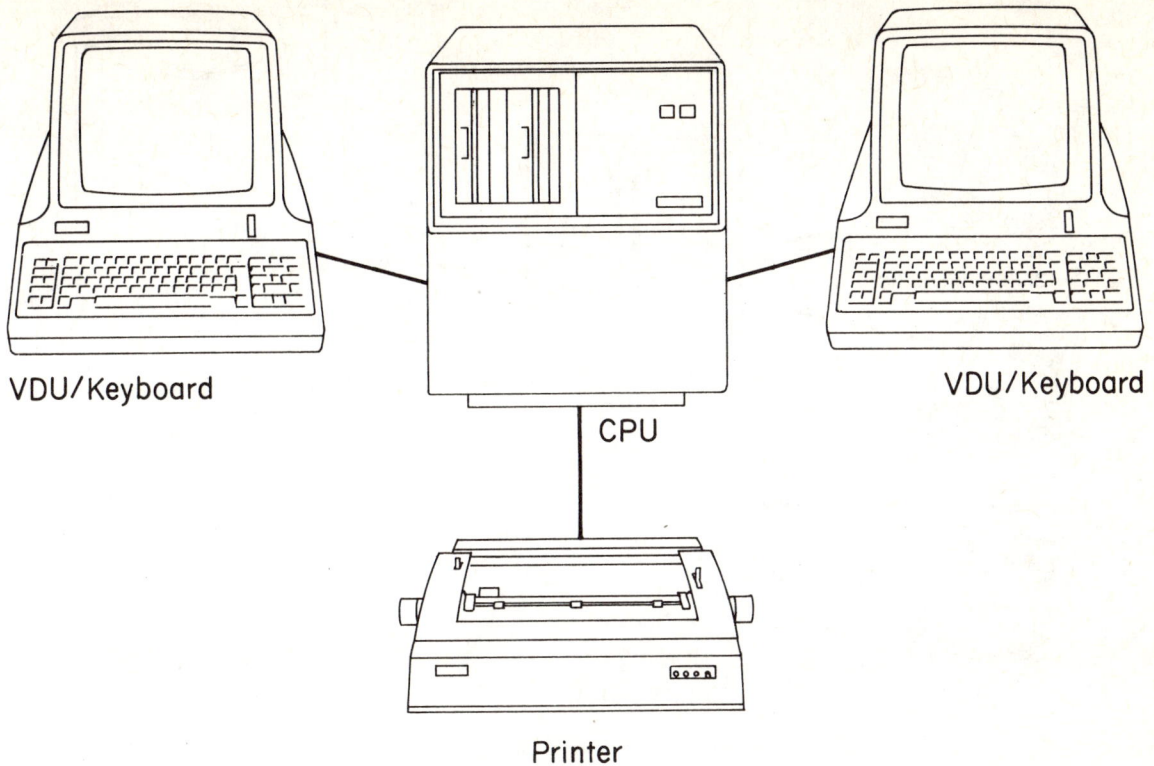

Fig 18 Shared-logic system

Mainframe systems

Taking shared-logic a stage further, the central processor may be an existing mainframe computer (Figure 19), also being used for data processing simultaneously with the word-processing function.

It is possible for a mainframe system to work on a time-sharing basis. In this instance the computer is owned and maintained by a bureau or co-operative, and the individual users are equipped with relatively inexpensive terminals. User-access to the computer is through a communications network and time is metered and paid for in much the same way as the telephone. In this way, the capital cost of the equipment is spread over a large number of users.

Word processing and data processing are coming ever closer and systems are being developed which are designed to combine the two uses in shared-logic, or even stand-alone systems.

Communicating word processors It is a natural extension of the shared-logic idea that the various component units do not necessarily have to be in the same building. It does not matter to a computer whether the cable joining it to the keyboard and VDU comes from the other side of the room, or the other side of the world. Using existing telephone networks or custom-built data networks – particularly as the use of optical fibres to replace copper cable increases – there is no reason why word-processors

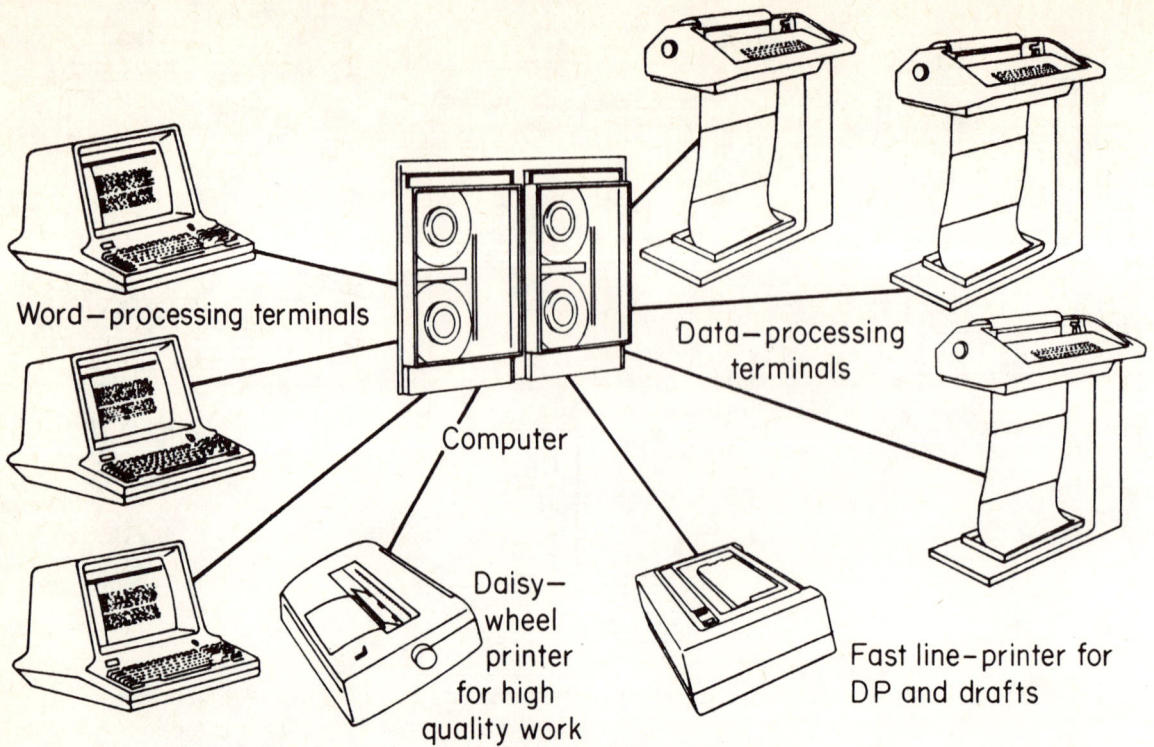

Fig 19 Mainframe system

should not communicate with each other quite happily over long distances. Digital code is digital code, and, as long as the same 'language' is used from the limited selection available, it is quite possible that a letter typed on the VDU of one company may be printed out, seconds later, in the office of another.

A dynamic situation   The dynamic situation which exists in microelectronics in general, and office equipment in particular, renders inevitable the fact that new developments will have taken place while this book is being printed. For this reason, the author has tried to consider broad principles rather than the detail of how they are carried out.

It is unlikely that any new advances will in the short term invalidate the concept of 'keyboard – screen – central processor – printer' for the first-time production of text or data. Control and command mechanisms will develop with an increasing use of the 'mouse' for non-keyboarding users. This is a hand-held device which is moved over the desk-top to control the cursor, and indicate which of a number of options – probably pictorially represented – are required. Voice-recognition will replace keyed-in command sequences in many systems. When developments in memory capacity permit, full voice-input from the originator's dictation will become a possibility. The three basic forms of memory will continue to be used, though probably improved out of all recognition.

Progress inevitably makes liars of all those who write of 'the present' or 'the future'. It is to be hoped however, that this chapter will have achieved – and will continue to achieve – its objective of bringing about a better understanding of what constitutes a word processor.

4 What does it do?

The basic functions

This chapter and the following one, 'How does it do it?' assume a stand-alone configuration consisting of keyboard, VDU displaying 80 characters wide, central processor with floppy disks, and a letter-quality printer. The system is either a dedicated word processor or computer with a 'user-friendly' word processing software package. It is not practicable to cope with the many and varied WP packages in great detail, but an attempt has been made to indicate where alternative methods are likely to be used. The intention is to state in broad outline what might be *expected* from a word processor in terms of functions and ability. The actual operation of the equipment is covered in the next chapter

Setting out the page The equipment is typically programmed by inserting a program – or 'software' – disk and allowing it to run for a short period of time until there is an indication, audible or visual, that programming is complete. Depending upon the system used, information will appear at the top or bottom of the screen showing 'default values' of the various settings concerned with page design. There will probably be a 'ruler line' or 'format line' relating to the horizontal scale on a typewriter, indicating margins and tab settings. There will also be information about the width and length of the page, and linespacing and pitch to be used when printing out. The 'standard page' presented by the program may not in fact be a workable page. It may simply be a starting-point, or an indication of the upper or lower limits for any particular setting. The status – or information – lines on the screen will also show prompts and error messages during operation of the system, and probably indicate the name and page number if any, of the current document in use. To summarise, the information shown in the status lines will probably contain the following:

> The 'mode', or kind of operation which is to be carried out
> The maximum width of the page in characters
> Lines per page
> The length of the paper upon which the page is to be printed
> The number of lines to be left blank at the top of the page
> Line-spacing
> Pitch
> Margin settings

Mode Literally, a method, or way of acting. The system is instructed to behave in a certain manner until further notice. For example, *MODE UNDERLINE* will cause text to be underlined as it is typed; *MODE HYPHEN* will select suitable hyphenation points. Some systems require the operator to enter an 'edit mode' before corrections can be carried out.

Pitch The number of characters to the inch that will be printed. The choice may vary from a simple 10 or 12 to a wide range from 3 to 40 characters per inch. As the measurements relating to page width, margins and tabs are all in *characters,* the pitch chosen will affect the actual linear measurement in inches, so this should be determined at an early stage.

Line-spacing   The number of lines to the inch is usually expressed in typewriter terms as single, 1½ or double spacing. Single line-spacing is 6 lines to the inch. The spacing available may vary according to the printer and software used, from a choice of 1, 1½ or 2, to a total flexibility of choice in increments of as little as one-eighth of a linespace (one forty-eighth of an inch). The number of lines which it is possible to print on the page will depend upon the linespacing setting so this too should be determined at an early stage.

Page width   This is the width of the actual paper on which the copy will be printed, and may or may not require a specific setting. Some systems simply set the margins.

Page or form length   This again is the length of the actual paper which is to be used. It is necessary in cases where a sheet-feeder is fitted, to ensure that each page begins printing at the same position. It may also be a necessary part of automatic repagination where this takes account of varying linespacing within a page.

Lines per page   This is the number of lines which will be contained in a page on the screen during initial input, regardless of the line-spacing setting. When the specified number of lines has been typed, the system will either warn the operator of this fact or the system may generate an 'automatic page-break' in the form of a line across the screen. Print, file and cursor movement commands will take account of these 'page breaks' and will usually only operate upon the page in which the cursor is placed at the time of the command.

Margins and tabs   These are usually set in the 'ruler' or 'format' line. Both left and right margins may be shown, or in order to ensure the longest possible typing line being displayed, the left margin may take the form of a 'print offset'. In this case, the left margin is in effect the left-hand side of the screen, and the print offset ensures that printing starts a specified number of characters from the left of the paper. Some systems are capable of working with multiple margin settings, enabling text or figures to be entered and edited in column format. Without this facility, if text is typed in columns to tab settings, editing one column will usually affect the alignment of succeeding columns to the right.

Tabs are also set in the ruler line. The program may set 'default tabs' at intervals which can be either used or changed at will. Most systems also allow the setting of special 'align tabs' for entering figures in columns. The decimal points will align below the tab. Where there is an arithmetic capability in the word-processing program, the setting of align tabs also serves to identify the columns of figures by number.

Offset   Sometimes known as the 'top margin', this is the number of lines which the printer will wind up before beginning to print. This is expressed in lines, and may be used, for example, to print on letter-headed paper. Where no offset is permitted, the same effect may be obtained by inserting blank lines or carriage-returns at the top of the page.

Storing page
formats
Most word-processing systems will allow empty pages consisting only of format settings to be stored on disk. An operator can therefore store all the page settings for her most commonly-used jobs, and call each one back as it is required. Some systems will not allow empty pages to be stored. In this case it is only necessary to type a single character on the screen, which can then be filed as a page. When the page format is required again, the page is recalled, and the character deleted. It may be necessary to create a 'page' before being able to type on the screen. Alternatively you may be able to type in the 'default' page, and determine the final setting when the document is completed.

Typing on the
screen
Let us assume that you are typing a completely new document, starting with a blank screen. Having set all your margins and so on, you will see a signal, which usually but not always will flash so as to be more easily found on a page of text. It may be in the form of an underscore, a reversed-out rectangle in which the characters appear as a 'negative' of their usual colouring, or as some other symbol, according to make and type of machine.

The cursor
This is called the cursor, and moves as you type, always indicating the position of the _next_ character. You will learn to use this cursor in a number of ways – to define text, or perhaps move it. But for the moment let it simply show you where you are. You can always find the cursor quickly, even among a mass of type, as its position is duplicated at the top of the screen.

Word
wraparound
When you are typing on a word processor, you do not have to worry about stopping in time at the end of each line and using a carriage-return to move to the beginning of the next. The machine does it all for you. In effect you just type a single continuous line of text.

What happens if the end of the line comes in the middle of a word? This is where a process called 'word-wraparound' comes into effect. Every time you operate the space-bar to insert a space between words, you type what is known as a 'written space' – as opposed to a blank space, which is what the screen is full of when you start. A 'written space' is a _character_ as far as the machine is concerned, and is subject to all the rules which govern characters. At the end of each line as the right-hand margin is reached the machine 'looks back' along the line. If the last character to be typed was a written space, the machine moves to the beginning of the next line and carries on from there. If there is _no_ written space telling the machine that a word has been completed, it searches back along the line until it finds one – at the end of the previous word. It then transfers everything after that space to the beginning of the next line. If you see that this is likely to happen at an unsuitable point, in the middle of a date or a name for example, you can insert a 'required join' which will mean that the whole of the date or name will be treated as one word, and moved to the next line in its entirety. Alternatively, you may need to mark the beginning and end of the words which are to be tied together, which has the same effect.

Underlining
You may be able to underline in three ways depending on your machine. First you can underline just as you would on a typewriter. Second, you can instruct

the machine to underline a whole block of text – from a single word to a whole page – *after* it has been typed, or you can instruct the machine in advance and it will underline every character as you go.

Capitals Single capital letters may be typed by using the shift key, just as on a typewriter. Most word processors will also have a shift lock, which will put the entire keyboard into upper-case. Some machines also have a capitals 'mode' which will type all the letters in upper-case, but leave figures and symbols in lower-case. The shift key will of course act normally on the unaffected characters. This is useful for typing capitals and numbers combined, as in parts-identification numbers, or registration numbers.

Emboldening To add emphasis to a word or heading, instead of resorting to the usual underlining, you can embolden the type. To do this, the machine when printing will print each character normally, then shift very slightly to the right and print it again, thus producing a heavier outline. Some systems allow varying degrees of emboldening, depending upon the number of times the characters are over-printed. The bold print may not appear on the screen, but will be indicated by a distinctive symbol which will appear before and after the text which is thus treated. Some systems however are capable of displaying emboldened type on the screen.

Sub- and superscript If mathematical or chemical formulae are to be typed, figures or letters can be printed above or below the normal typing line as required. The amount by which the characters are elevated or depressed will depend on the method used. Using one method, the amount is fixed at one quarter space above or below the line. A second method allows the amount to be controlled by the operator.

Vertical alignment When typing columns of figures, particularly if monetary sums or decimal points are involved, the method used is to set special tabs or alignment marks. After the cursor is moved to an *alignment tab,* the characters will enter from right to left. Each successive character occupies the position immediately to the left of the align tab and, as each new character is typed, any characters already typed move aside to the left, as they do when you enter figures into a calculator.

Vertical alignment may also be used for right-ranging text as for example when typing a date which is to line up with the right margin. The characters will enter similarly, each displacing the previous one to the left.

Running corrections These are corrections carried out on the typist's own initiative, usually to rectify keying errors such as mis-keying, omissions, or accidentally-struck extra characters. They can also result from misreading of copy, skipping whole lines, or typing a word twice as the result of a break in continuity. When using a normal typewriter, such errors usually involve the use of erasers, correcting fluid, paper, or correcting ribbon. If the error concerns more than one or two characters, it may well involve retyping the entire page. With a word processor, these errors are almost as easy to correct as they are to make. Correction is carried out on the VDU screen before the text is committed to paper, and there is no visible sign to indicate that an error was ever made.

Mis-keyed characters	On some systems these are corrected simply by committing the typist's cardinal sin of overtyping. The cursor is positioned below the character to be replaced, and the correct character keyed in. On others, the unwanted character must be erased or deleted before the correct one is typed.

Remember that a 'written space' produced by either the space-bar or the backspace key *is*, as far as the machine is concerned, a character. You can therefore *erase* characters very easily by overtyping them with written space. Bear in mind, however, that the remaining text will not close up to fill a gap composed of written spaces, because to the machine no gap exists. To remove quantities of text, you will probably use the 'delete' function, described in the next section.

Deleting text	This is not the same as erasing, as just described, in which the characters are replaced with written spaces. When characters are *deleted*, only blank spaces remain, and the following text will close up. You can delete single characters one at a time, or you can define whole blocks of text for deletion as lines, words, sentences, paragraphs or otherwise, depending on the system used.

Erasing text	As well as erasing characters singly by using the space-bar or backspace key, you may be able to use an erase command to remove whole blocks or lines of text. This operation will replace *all* the erased characters with written spaces, so the remaining text will not close up. The erase feature can be selective, for example removing underlining, but leaving the underlined characters intact. Where a 'graphics' feature is available, it may be possible for either the characters or graphics to be erased without affecting the other.

Inserting text	Omitted or additional text can be easily inserted – an operation almost invariably calling for a complete retype when a typewriter is being used. Using one method, when the 'command sequence' for insertion is begun, all the text following the point where the insertion is to commence drops down by one line to leave room for the insertion. If the matter to be inserted goes beyond the end of the line upon which it was started, the remaining text will continue to drop away, a line at a time, until the insertion is completed. On conclusion of the operation, 'word-wraparound' takes place, and the text rearranges itself to follow on from the insertion.

On other systems, insertion is simply a matter of positioning the cursor where the insertion is to begin, and typing the new material. The new text 'elbows' the old out of the way, creating its own space as it goes. Some of the less sympathetic WP packages on microcomputers require the point of insertion to be marked by codes. The new material is then typed elsewhere on the screen, and the insertion assembled by means of a further command.

You must always remember to 'write' a space with the space-bar at the end of an insertion or the text will close right up to the end of the last word.

Hyphenating	When word-wraparound takes place, either at the end of each line during normal typing or when text closes up after an adjustment, it may leave unsightly gaps at

the ends of lines where long words have been carried over to the next line. You may wish to reduce these gaps by hyphenating the carried-over word. This can be done in two ways. The easiest is to wait until all other corrections and editing operations have been completed. If you do *not* do this, any subsequent action which results in word-wraparound will destroy all the hyphenation and you will have to start all over again. When you are sure that no further text movement will take place, you may be able to select a hyphenation 'mode'. This will take each line in turn, and offer a suggested hyphenation point based on the number of spaces to be filled. This suggestion can be accepted as it stands; modified by the operator, or the word can be rejected as being unsuitable for hyphenation.

Text revision
This is usually carried out upon the instructions of the originator after he has edited a draft. It may involve deleting, erasing or inserting text as already described, or he may call for headings to be centred, text indented from one or both sides, or whole blocks of text to be reformatted or moved about within the page, of from one page to another.

Centring text
Normally a laborious typewriting task, this can now be achieved by pressing only a few keys. Words, lines, or whole blocks of text can be centred. This last feature may be useful where such things as menus, lists of speakers and so on are to be typed, but remember that when centring a *block* of text, *every line* will be centred and the alignment of the left-hand margin destroyed.

Indenting paragraphs
You may be able to indent existing paragraphs either from the left or right margin, or from both simultaneously. When you do this, the lines within the paragraph become shorter, and a kind of reverse word wraparound takes place. The words for which there is no longer sufficient room on the first line are pushed to the next, and these in turn displace further words, and a 'waterfall' of words continues until new lines are formed to accommodate the surplus at the end of the paragraph. This in turn makes the paragraph *longer,* and so any remaining text on the page has to move down to make room for it. You will realise from this that the amount of indentation may depend on whether or not there is space at the *bottom* of the page – a fact not always realised by editing authors.

Defining a quantity of text
If you wish to operate in some way upon a quantity of text, either deleting, erasing, underlining, justifying or moving it, you must first *define* the text which you wish to change. The definition may be descriptive that is Word, Line, Paragraph; or it may be an indicated block of text. A block may be a Text Quantity, which is a linear amount commencing and finishing at specified points such as a sentence, or it may be a rectangular area of the screen, whatever it contains. Whatever the quantity of text defined, it will usually be identified on the screen by a half-tone effect which covers the affected characters while still allowing them to be read. Thus you can check before completing the operation that the correct quantity has been defined.

Moving text
The ability to move text on the screen varies widely from system to system. Using advanced equipment, you can move a line, or a number of lines, up or down a page. The remainder of text on the page will readjust around the moved text. If, for example, you wish to transpose two adjacent paragraphs by defining

the second one and simply moving it up to its new position, the deposed text will move down to the position vacated by the first paragraph, and the transposition is complete. On this type of system you may also be able to move a column of figures to the right or left.

On less advanced equipment you will need to use a 'putaside' or buffer memory as described in the next section to store text temporarily before inserting it in a new position.

Putaside You may want to remove a block of text temporarily, simply to put it out of the way while you do something else. Perhaps you want to rearrange the rest of the page, or change the shape of the graphics where they exist, or even move the text to another page. In order to do this, you have what is called a 'putaside' or buffer memory. This is a section of the main memory of the processor, which allows you to store characters on a short-term basis, and recall them to the screen during the current term of use of the machine. As the characters are stored in the main memory and not on a disk they will be lost if the machine is switched off. Any operation requiring the use of the putaside memory must be completed before the end of the working day, or alternatively the characters must be recalled and transferred to more permanent storage on disk if the job has to be continued the following day. You may put aside any defined quantity of text, from a single character up to the capacity of the putaside memory. When recalling from putaside to the screen, care must be taken that the recalled text will not over-write any already displayed.

Depending upon the system used, some will automatically *insert* recalled text, and existing text will be merely displaced. Others will arbitrarily place the recalled text in the position indicated by cursor or code, erasing any material which is already occupying that space. Where a 'graphics' feature is available, the putaside memory may usefully be employed to duplicate 'boxes' for ticks or replies to questions.

Making up a vocabulary The putaside memory can often be used for storing a number of long, difficult or frequently-used words or phrases. These can then be recalled and inserted into the text by simply keying-in the number of the line upon which the term has been stored. Imagine that you are, for example, a medical secretary working for a number of consultants in different branches of medicine. You could create a vocabulary for each consultant consisting of the most frequently-used terms in the particular area concerned. These vocabularies would be stored permanently on disk, but whenever you were working for a particular consultant you would recall the appropriate vocabulary page to the screen, and then consign it to the putaside memory. If the term 'cardio-vascular' is on line four of the vocabulary, you can type the whole word by keying the number 4 together with the correct command keys.

Replacing character strings This is the automatic, or semi-automatic replacement of one specified character-string with another throughout an entire document. A character-string is an *exact* specification of the characters, symbols and spaces which make up a word or phrase.

'Word-processor' for example is not the same as 'word processor'. The fact that one has a hyphen and one does not means that, to the machine, they are different words. If a word which is to be replaced is likely to occur at the beginning of a sentence with a capital, and also in the body of a sentence without a capital, the word must be defined in both forms, and so must the word which is to replace it. In defining a 'search-string' – that is a character-string for which you are going to ask the machine to search – you must be precise.

Some systems will allow you the choice of differentiating between upper and lower case. You may, for example, be able to ask the machine to look for a word or combination of words irrespective of capital letters. Having found the words in question, the system will then replace them in whatever form by a precisely-specified alternative. This can be extremely useful to authors who are required by their publishers to standardise the use of capitals in certain words – as I have found to my delight in the past. Alternatively, you may be able to specify that a word is replaced *only* when found in a certain form, and not otherwise. The colour brown, for example, would remain unchanged if you had asked the machine to search only for the surname Brown, with a capital B.

You may be able to specify that the character-string is only replaced when found as a complete word. If not, you must also consider whether that particular combination of letters is likely to occur as part of another word. If for instance you were to take the manuscript of this book and ask the processor to replace the verb 'type' with the more up-to-date 'keyboard' you might find yourself reading about 'keyboardwriters' – 'protokeyboards' – 'keyboardfaces' or particular keyboards of people or equipment. To prevent this happening, you would need to include a written space before and after the word 'type' when defined as a search string. This would of course mean that the spaces which occurred before and after each separate word 'type' would be erased along with the word, so you would also write a space at each end of the replacement word to rectify this.

You may have two possible methods of searching and replacing available to you. In one, the processor will replace a single search-string with another on the displayed page by indicating each occurrence of the search-string in turn. The operator then has the option of replacing or not on each and every occasion. The second and much more powerful method can replace a number of character-strings simultaneously throughout a document consisting of many pages. This method usually occupies the VDU screen, and so the operator cannot use it for anything else during the course of the operation.

Filing As well as temporarily holding a great deal of information in the main memory of the central processing unit, the word processor will also store information, permanently if required, on discrete media. Discrete media in various systems take the form of tapes, magnetic cards or various forms of disk. These are mainly magnetic media and 'discrete' means that they can be removed from the machine and transported or stored away from it. You will see that the use of such discrete media storage increases the capacity of the word processor to an infinite degree, as there is no limit to the number of tapes, cards or disks which can be stored separately.

The work disks   Most word processors have two 'disk drives' and can use two work disks at the same time. Some systems have two disk drives, but one is permanently occupied by the program disk, so only one work disk can be inserted. The work disks most commonly used are 'floppy disks' and each can hold typically about 300 000 characters but technology is constantly improving to increase the capacity. The way in which text is stored depends upon whether the system is 'page-oriented' or 'document-oriented'. Both methods have their advocates, and both undoubtedly have their faults. A page-oriented system stores text on pages, roughly approximating to the final printed version. A piece of work comprising many pages may be given a single text-name or file-name, and each page given its own number and possibly an additional reference to remind the operator of its contents. Any page thus stored can then be recalled singly to the screen for further editing or printing-out.

In the example which follows, the file-name, or text-name, is 'Repreports', and the references are the names of the representatives, together with the page numbers:

REPREPORTS
(Smith) 1
(Jones) 2
(McTavish) 3
(Singh) 4
(Reilly) 5

CONFERENCE
(May) 1
(June) 2
(July) 3

As each page is created on the screen and then filed on the disk, an index is automatically recorded on the disk. When a work disk is inserted into the machine, the operator calls up the index to the screen first, by keying-in a command sequence. She then recalls the page which she requires, by keying-in the text-name, and then the reference, for example, CONFERENCE (May) 1.

In a document-oriented system, more typical of the computer-style WP package than of the dedicated word processor, an entire document is stored under one name, however many printed pages which it contains. When this is recalled to the screen, the entire piece of work appears. The pages within the document may be indicated by 'page-breaks' in the form of lines across the screen. These are generated by the system whenever a specified number of lines has been typed. Alternatively, forced pagebreaks may be artificially induced for example, at the end of a chapter or section. To arrive at page 20 of such a document, the operator may need to scroll through pages 1 to 19, though some systems have a 'go to' key which enables the operator to go straight to the specified page. Repagination of such documents tends to be easier, as the page-breaks will simply reposition themselves during editing. Problems may arise however if there are changes in line-spacing within pages. It usually takes the added sophistication of the more advanced page-oriented software to ensure that every page occupies the same *space* on the printed page.

The capacity of a disk in number of pages will vary. It is determined in a page-oriented system by two things: the number of text-names used, and the actual amount of text on each page.

Say for example that the index on the disk can hold 128 entries. A *text-name* counts as one entry, and each *page number* counts as one entry. So, if all the pages on one disk were stored under one text-name, the capacity of the *index* would be 127 pages (128 less the one used for the textname). This then is the *maximum* number of pages you could ever get on one disk of this type, on this particular system. Each additional text-name used *reduces* the capacity of the disk in numbers of pages.

Now take the amount of text on each page. The maximum likely number of *characters* possible on one page is about 7500 (94 lines of 80 characters each). If, as is highly unlikely, you were to fill every page to its absolute maximum, about 40 pages of this size would account for the *total* capacity of the disk, amounting to 300 000 characters.

So you will see that the actual capacity in number of pages on a disk may vary between a *maximum* of 127 determined by the index, and a *minimum* of 40, dictated by the capacity of the disk in characters. In practice, it usually works out that a typical floppy disk will hold around 90–100 pages. When or shortly before a disk is full, a message appears on the screen to that effect.

Prompts All operations on a word processor are controlled by pressing certain keys in a prescribed order. This is known as a 'command sequence'. As some operations, particularly those associated with filing, require quite lengthy command sequences, the operator is helped through these by a series of messages which appear upon the VDU screen. These are called 'prompts'. They may ask the operator questions, such as 'TEXTNAME?' or 'OPTION?', at the same time stating what options are available to her. Or they may confirm exactly what it is that she has asked the machine to do, so that she can carry out a final check before pressing the last key in the sequence, which tells the machine to 'execute' or complete the operation. You will learn more about command sequences in the next chapter. Other kinds of prompts, sometimes referred to as 'error messages' warn the operator of malfunctions of the equipment, or of errors in operation producing 'illegal' commands. These usually indicate the kind of error or fault either in plain terms, or by a coded message explained in the instruction manual with the system. Examples of these might be 'INCOMPLETE' indicating that the instruction given lacked certain essential information, or 'S.10' referring to a software-induced fault in the equipment.

Opening a file When a new file is entered, or 'opened', all the formats, consisting of margins, tabs etc and the page description containing the width, length, number of lines and so on become part of the page, and return with it each time it is recalled to the screen. You need not necessarily file the whole of a document which is displayed on the screen. You may be able to set the cursor, and then instruct the machine to file only that which appears above, or below the cursor. If you had created a complicated form, using the 'graphics' feature to draw lines ruling it up, you could temporarily dispose of the text into the 'Putaside' memory, and then file the remaining skeleton for future use for that text and other texts. You may also remember that you can file an empty page consisting only of the format and page description, so that you can type letters in the house style, or any other frequently-used layout, without needing to set up the display afresh each time.

Updating a file You can update a file by recalling it to the screen, making the necessary changes, and then re-entering it in place of the original version. However, this destroys the original version, and so is not always the most appropriate method. If you wish to retain the original, perhaps to use again many times in amended form, you will open the new pages on the disk under new text-names or document names, thereby leaving the original unchanged.

Some machines update automatically without reference to the operator during normal text-editing. This is known for obvious reasons as 'destructive editing' and usually means that the equipment does not have sufficient memory capacity to contain both old and new versions simultaneously. To retain the original version of a document when using such a system. It is necessary to make a copy before beginning to edit, then to work only on one or the other version, leaving the other unchanged.

Deleted pages file On some systems, when you update a file, or delete a file because it is no longer required, the machine puts a copy of that page into a special 'deleted pages' file on the disk. If you then realise that you have updated or deleted the wrong file, you can recall the original from the deleted pages file as long as it remains there. *You* decide the size of this file. If you decide that a safety margin of five pages is required, you open a deleted pages file of that number of pages on every new disk. Each time you delete or update a file, a copy goes into the deleted pages file until it is full. From that point on, each new entry displaces the oldest one in the file. On other systems, if you open a new file with the same text-name as an existing one, the machine automatically creates a 'backup' file, retaining the original in case of accident or error.

Building-blocks One of the most commonly-known and frequently-cited uses of a word processor is writing letters which consist of standard paragraphs. These are referred to as 'building-blocks'. In the United States, this operation is called 'boiler-plating'. To do this, the text is split up into numbered blocks by coded signals, and recalled to the screen as required by keying-in the text-name, page, and number of the block.

Deleting outdated files When you have finished with material which is recorded on disk, and are sure that it will not be required in the future, you should delete it, otherwise the disks are going to become full up with useless material. Page-oriented systems will allow you to delete individual pages or whole files; document-oriented systems will only allow deletion of entire documents. Some systems will allow entire disks to be cleared in a single operation, others insist on documents or files being deleted individually. In some cases, 'deleting' a file from the disk merely means that the index entry for that file is removed. The actual content of the file remains on the disk until it is overwritten by new material. Hence, even if the system does not have a deleted pages or 'dustbin' file, it may be possible to retrieve 'lost' text by means of a special salvage program.

Creating duplicate master files As a further precaution against losing important text such as lengthy or complicated contracts or other legal documents or similar material, you must copy these on to a 'backup' disk which is then kept in a safe place away from your normal stock of working disks. If there are two disk drives in the word processor, you can copy from one disk to the other.

Reorganising files If you have a page-oriented system, you will probably be able to move pages around within files, or from one file to another. For example, you may wish to change the order of pages within a file. When you have done so, the pages may appear in the index in the changed order but still bearing their original page numbers; they may be renumbered but remain in their old positions, or they may be moved and renumbered, depending upon the system in use.

An experienced operator will often change the name of a file temporarily if it is going to be extensively edited or otherwise worked upon. By renaming the file as, say, 'x', the operator can save many keystrokes which would have been required to recall the file by its full text-name. When the operation is complete, a further change will restore the original text-name.

Pagination The term pagination is used by different manufacturers to denote splitting a document into separate pages by the insertion of 'page breaks'; the numbering of pages, or the readjustment of page-length after extensive editing. This last is often more accurately referred to as 'repagination'. In this, the pages are adjusted so as to be the same length. The more powerful systems are able to take account of variations in line-spacing within a page, thus ensuring that the text on each page occupies the same amount of *space,* measured in single-spacing. Others content themselves with allotting the same number of typed lines to every page. You may be able to choose whether the operation is to be carried out completely automatically – in which case it will occupy the screen but the printer can be used for something else – or whether it will adopt a semi-automatic method of operation. In this case the machine will display each page in turn, and wait for you to approve it before going on to the next.

Several things could go wrong during pagination: for example, you might find a page beginning with the last line of a paragraph, or ending with the first line of a paragraph. These are known in the printing trade as 'widows' and there is a special option available which will vary the set number of lines so that the 'widow' is moved to the page containing the rest of the paragraph. Another problem is where you have two or more lines which must remain together – a literary quotation perhaps – at the end of a page. You can avoid splitting these by using a 'required join' code. You can use required joins to connect as many lines as you wish. If the number of lines so joined exceeds the capacity of a page, the entire block will be moved to the next page.

Headers and footers Most word processors will allow you to add headers and footers during the printing of a multi-page document. These are running headings such as chapter or section titles which are to be repeated at the head or foot of every page. To type these during the initial keying-in would mean that if extensive editing was carried out involving insertion, deletion or moving of large blocks of text, the headers and footers would be displaced into the body of the text. It is therefore only possible for the printer to add these *after* the final repagination. A header or footer may also contain special coding which will number pages automatically during printing.

Printing Printing on the word processor is probably the easiest of all the various operations. In fact, once you have given the correct instructions to the CPU, which controls the printer just as it controls everything else, you can just sit back and let it happen. Or you can get on with the next job, because printing on most word processors is a 'background' operation. This means that if you are printing from material filed on a disk, you can at the same time use the keyboard and VDU to prepare further work.

The printer resembles a typewriter without a keyboard as you can see in Figure 20. The platen, paper bail, paper guides and release are not much different from those on an ordinary single-element electric or electronic typewriter.

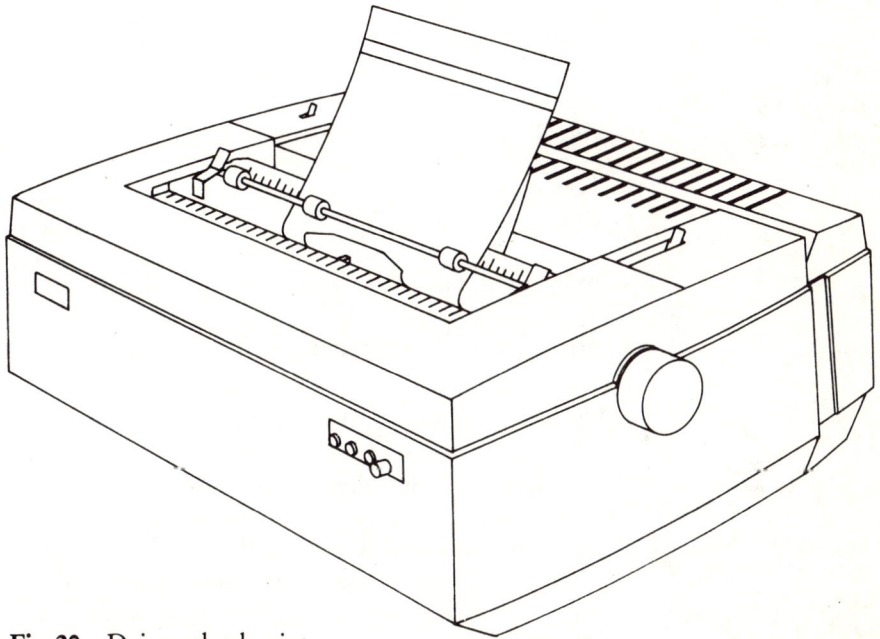

Fig 20 Daisy-wheel printer

Single sheets of paper, with copy flimsies and carbon paper if required, are fed into the machine by hand in the normal way, or by means of an automatic 'hopper feed' (see p.51) which inserts single pages, or packs, from a bulk supply. Hopper feeds are available either for single-sheet feeding, or can use both headed paper and continuation sheets. Some will also cope with envelopes. If continuous stationery is to be used, a special 'tractor feed' is fitted. This consists of toothed wheels or sprockets, which engage with holes punched down the sides of the continuous forms. The stationery is folded concertina-fashion, and placed on a tray to the rear of the printer. Completed work is automatically stacked on a second tray.

Pitch Whereas an ordinary typewriter will offer a single pitch, usually 10 or 12 characters to the inch and an electronic typewriter may give you the choice of 10, 12 or 15 cpi, some word-processor printers are capable of a wide range of pitches, from as few as 3 to 40 or more cpi. Some are software-driven – that is to say that changes of pitch can be effected by codes embedded in the text; others have switches on the printer. Variations in pitch are to a certain extent limited by the availability of suitable printwheels. Figures 21 and 22 show the effect of printing in different pitches with both 10 and 12-pitch wheels. See in particular how the 12-pitch wheel can print at 13 cpi without any noticeable deterioration, but when 15-pitch is used, the characters begin to run together. Printwheels are available for 10, 12, 15 and 20 pitch.

```
This is a ten-pitch wheel printing at 10 pitch

a ten-pitch wheel printing at 8 pitch

ch wheel printing at 6 pitch

i n g     a t     3     p i t c h
```

Fig 21   Ten-pitch print wheel

```
This is a twelve-pitch wheel printing at 12 pitch

This is a twelve-pitch wheel printing at 13 pitch

This is a twelve-pitch wheel printing at 15 pitch
```

Fig 22   Twelve-pitch print wheel

Control codes   Line-spacing is controlled by the format recorded on the disk with each page, as are margin settings, tabs and so on. The printer is actually controlled by codes recorded on the disk along with the text. These codes can be seen in the form of various symbols on the VDU screen, each denoting a carriage return, stop, justify or one of the many other special codes. Although these symbols are clearly visible on the screen, and serve as a useful means of checking that a correct instruction has been recorded, they are not themselves printed. An exception to this rule is that when numbered blocks of text are set up for 'Block building' construction of standard letters, the operator may be able to instruct the machine to type a copy of the page *including* the block numbers, for use as a reference when compiling the letters.

Methods of printing   You may be able to print in three ways, directly from the keyboard, from the VDU display, or from the files.

Printing from the keyboard   You can if you wish use some word processors just like a typewriter. As you type, the characters appear on the screen and are simultaneously printed out on to paper. The automatic carriage-return at the end of each line may not work when you are printing from the keyboard, so you may have to set a 'bell zone' to warn you of the approach of the end of each line, then use the carriage-return key as you would on a typewriter.

Printing from the screen   Some systems will allow you to print directly from the screen without filing the page on a disk. While you are doing this, the screen is occupied, and cannot be used for anything else.

Printing from the files   This is the method which you will normally find yourself using. Consider that it is but the work of seconds to file a page from the screen. When you have done so, not only do you have a permanent record of the page for use in subsequent editing operations, but in most cases you also enable the printer to work 'in background', thereby freeing the keyboard and screen for more useful work. You may be able to instruct the printer to print a single page, or a number of pages in sequence under a single text-name. If you are using single sheets of paper, the printer will automatically stop at the end of each page for you to insert a new sheet. Using continuous stationery, the machine will move on to each fresh sheet in turn, and will also print as many copies of each page as you instruct it to. These will of course all be 'top copies' of equal quality, unlike deteriorating carbon copies.

Stacking print-jobs   On the more powerful systems, you can 'stack' or 'queue' printing jobs, and the machine will carry them out in sequence. This can only be done of course if you are using continuous stationery, or a hopper feed for single sheets or sets. It means, however, that you can set the printer several tasks to do while you are working out a complicated document on the screen, or doing other work away from the machine.

Fig 23   A hopper feed

There are a number of options which may be offered to you during printing. When printing directly from the screen, you can on some systems position the cursor, and then instruct the machine to print only that which is above or below it. As already mentioned, you may be able to ask the printer to print the block numbers in addition to the text, in order to identify individual lines, or standard paragraphs.

You may also be able to ask for special codes which are not normally printed, or text typed in the margins to be printed out for reference purposes.

Justifying margins Most printers will justify the right-hand margin. The last character on each line will be printed in the same character position, immediately before the right-hand margin. The adjustments are made by altering the spaces between words, so before justifying it is usually necessary to hyphenate in order to remove any long gaps at the ends of lines. Failure to do this will result in disproportionately large spaces between words spoiling the appearance of the line. The text displayed on the screen will not in most cases be justified, so the final result will not be seen until it is printed out.

Index For ease of identification or reference purposes, some systems allow you to ask for the Index entry for each page to be printed at the head of the page. This will consist of the text-name, reference of any, and page number.

Varying line-spacing and pitch Normally the line-spacing and pitch will remain the same throughout a page, and will be as indicated on the status line on screen. If you wish to vary either of these within a page, you may be able to do so. You may for example wish to include in a letter or report an extract from an official document, or other published source. By reducing the line-spacing and/or pitch, and perhaps indenting the paragraph, the extract will stand out clearly from the remainder of the text. The change of spacing or pitch will not of course show as such on the screen, but codes in the text will tell the operator that the correct instructions will be given to the printer.

Merging text You can use the word processor to produce highly-personalised letters, such as those from a well-known publication assuring you that you have been specially selected . . . not only does the salutation of the letter contain your name, but the body of the letter is also liberally sprinkled with references to the district in which you live, plus repeated appeals to you by name. In order to do this, the basic letter is recorded in one file, with coded signals at all the points where a personalised variable will appear. In a second file is recorded a mailing list of 'specially-selected' recipients. Against each name is recorded the variables peculiar to that person. If, for example, you are Joan Smith, and live at 10 Laburnum Grove, Witchwood, Anytown, the variables are coded in with your name could include 'Joan' or 'M/s Smith' and 'Witchwood'. The letter beginning 'Dear Joan', and referring in one or more places to 'Witchwood' makes you feel that someone has really taken the trouble to find out all about you and where you live.

When you are producing such a mailing, you may be able to check that the system is working correctly by recalling both the text and the first set of variables to the screen. When you have reassured yourself that the finished result is as it should be, you then set the system into motion and the machine will proceed to work its way through the entire list. You can also use the same list to type the envelopes or labels so the whole operation is virtually automatic.

Page headings and numbering *(side heading, italic)*

Page headings and numbering If you open a printed book at random, you will usually find that the left-hand page and the right-hand page have different headings, according to the style of the publisher. In some books, the left-hand (verso) page will carry the title of the book and the right-hand (recto) page the title of the chapter. In others, the verso page carries the chapter headings and the recto page sub- or section headings. These are known as 'headers', and you can programme the word processor to print these on correctly alternating pages, by merging the text on one page with the header on another. You may prefer, or be instructed, that this information be at the bottom of the page rather than the top. The process is similar, but now they are called 'footers'. You can use either a header or a footer to number each page automatically as it is printed. This does not detract from the ability to head or foot each page, as up to four headers and footers can be used.

Sorting If you have the appropriate software, and the system is sufficiently powerful you can sort lists of names or words into alphabetical, numerical, or chronological order. Lists may be sorted in ascending or descending order, and a number of columns of text can be sorted simultaneously on the more powerful systems.

Selecting Again, subject to availability of software and memory capacity, you may be able to ask the machine to extract lists of words according to whatever information you have filed. If you had filed a complete list of personnel or students, with addresses, district, job-titles, qualifications, subjects taken or whatever other information you chose to put into the memory of the machine you could, in a short time, call to the screen a list of all personnel with certain qualifications or characteristics. This list could then be printed out for the benefit of prospective employers, promotions boards, or for timetabling purposes.

The list need not necessarily be the names of people. It could equally well be properties for sale, with details of values and districts, or motor vehicles held in stock, or holiday lettings, or anything else which could be selected by broad type or classification.

Arithmetic By adding on arithmetic package to the software options, some word processors become data processors. Basic calculations can then be applied to whole columns or lines of figures. A price list which is subject to a percentage increase across the board can be updated completely automatically. Alternatively, calculator-style operations in the basic four functions can be carried out.

Keystroke memory Some of the more advanced systems have a 'keystroke-memory' capacity which enables a series of keystrokes, which can be text-entry or commands, to be stored in the machine's memory. By combining the keystroke memory and arithmetic functions, strings of complicated calculations can be carried out with little effort. This facility may also be used for repetitive text-editing operations where, for example, a number of pages need to be reformatted. In some cases, stored keystrokes may be transferred to more permanent storage on disk, and recalled whenever they are required.

Additions to the system

These then, are just some of the things you can do with a word processor. By adding to it, or using peripheral equipment, you can produce punched paper tape for use with Telex or phototypesetters, or you can connect word processors to each other or to a larger computer. You can also arrange for two or more stand-alone processors to share a printer. Working as it does, at more than 500 wpm, it is unlikely that one operator could keep a printer fully employed, other than on block-building or standard-letter applications.

By using different programs, your word processor can become a computer which you can program yourself, if you are able, it can become a terminal to a computer-based information system such as the British Post Office's Prestel system; it can be used as the input to a phototypesetter or linked into a world-wide network of communicating equipment.

You will see from this that the word processor is a very versatile creature indeed, far removed from the simple editing typewriter or standard-letter writer that many people still imagine it to be. Now, for those who need to go more deeply into the methods by which all these things are achieved, in the next chapter we pass on to look at the construction and carrying out of command sequences.

5 How does it do it?

Building up a command sequence

This chapter is about giving instructions or 'commands' to a word processor. It sets out the basic principles of command sequences. We then go on to look at a selection of the special function keys which an operator may find in addition to the standard QWERTY layout on her keyboard; some of the codes and symbols which appear on the screen, and different procedures used for filing material on disk.

While it would be impossible to cover every eventuality for all makes and types of equipment, we have tried to set out in as general terms as possible most of the options which the operator will encounter.

Sequences will vary in detail from one make and type of word processor to another. Similarly, the keyboard shown in Figure 24 is a real one, but should only be used as an example of the *kind* of function keys which could be expected to exist in addition to the QWERTY keys. The intention here is to discuss the *principles* of giving instructions to a machine, not to train an operator.

As will be seen, the word processor or computer will not tolerate sloppy or imprecise commands. Exercises in making up simple command sequences may help to establish the habit of conveying instructions lucidly to other human beings, as well as to the microprocessor-based equipment.

A logical sequence Imagine for the moment that you are a teacher in charge of a class of thirty or so students, all with their heads down over some project or other. Suddenly you remark, out of the blue and to no one in particular, 'My word, it's turning chilly, I wish I had my cardigan. I left it in the staff-room at lunch-time. I wonder if one of you would be kind enough to fetch it for me? Jenny, you seem to have finished – would you be a dear?'

Jenny, far away in her own thoughts, comes to with a start at the sound of her name, but hasn't the faintest idea of what you want her to do. So you have to go through it all again. Now imagine the same request, but this time formulated rather differently. 'Jenny, will you do something for me? I want you to fetch my green cardigan from the staff-room on the top corridor. Right, off you go.'

This time Jenny is in no doubt as to what is required, and off she goes. Now let us look at the sequence of that instruction:

'Jenny' (Gains her attention)
'Will you do something for me?' (Warning of impending instruction)
'I want you to fetch (WHAT action is required)
my green cardigan (the SUBJECT of the action)
from the staff-room (the LOCATION of the subject)

Fig 24　A keyboard of a typical dedicated word processor

on the top corridor.
Right, off you go.' (Instruction to execute the action)

See the difference?

Now imagine that you have a word processor which we will call Fred, because as far as I know there are no word processors on the market with that name. You want Fred to delete a word which you have inadvertently typed twice:

'Fred, I want you to do something for me.'
'Your wish is my command, what do you want me to do?'
'I want you to delete something.'
'No problem, what?'
'A word.'
'OK, which word?'
'This word.'
'Got it!'
'Right, do it then.'

Now, because this is a simple and often-used sequence, we can dispense with the questions. So the sequence becomes:

'Fred, I want you to do something.'
'I want you to delete something.'
'A word.'
'This word.'
'Do it!'

Now substitute the operation of keys for the spoken word:

'Fred, I want you to do something.'   COMMAND
'I want you to delete something.'   DELETE
'A word.'   'W'
'This word.'   MOVE CURSOR
'Do it!'   EXECUTE

The cursor usually has to be positioned *before* the command sequence is started, so having done this, we are now left with:

COMMAND   **DELETE**   **W**   ⇦

command   delete   (W)ord   execute

. . . and this is a command sequence. It tells the machine, precisely and unequivocably, that you want it to delete a particular word.

Let us go back to Jenny for a moment. Supposing that upon arriving in the empty staff-room, she had chanced to see two green cardigans – one a pale green, obviously feminine garment, the other a chunky olive-green creation with leather patches and a tobacco-pipe sticking out of the pocket. Jenny, being a fairly bright girl, would be able to make an educated guess as to which was the right one. Not so your word processor. If insufficient information is given to enable it to know *exactly* what you want, it will either stop and display at the top of the screen a firm rebuke such as INCOMPLT or, even worse, ILLEGAL, or it will display a question asking for further information. The command sequence

COMMAND   DELETE   Ш   ⇦

follows the logical order of most command sequences, except that many are considerably longer and more involved. It tells the machine first that you want it to do something, then what it is, then specifies the amount of text to be affected. Then, when all the relevant information has been given, and checked from the displayed prompt line at the top of the screen, the command is executed.

As with all rules, there are exceptions. The information may not be required in exactly this order on every occasion; the sequence need not necessarily open with the COMMAND key, nor need it invariably finish with EXECUTE. To insert new text into an existing page for example, you may only need to key INSERT followed by the text you wish to add.

There are also a great many short cuts which can be taken by the experienced operator. Whole blocks of text can be moved by inserting spaces, instead of going through the command sequence which defines the amount of text to be moved. Paragraphs can be joined together and 'run on' simply by deleting the carriage returns between them. These, and many more simple ways of performing quite complicated tasks, are the hall-mark of the good operator. This is where the operator needs to be able to 'think on her feet' and select, perhaps from a number of options, the quickest, easiest and most efficient way of doing a particular job.

Before she can do this, however, she must be thoroughly trained in the operation of her own make and model of machine. All that this book is intended to do is to give an basic appreciation of the *principles* involved, and how many of them are applied. Let us take a look then, at some of the features which a word processor may offer its operator as a means of facilitating or cutting short some of the essential commands.

The keyboard   The keyboard illustrated in Figure 24 is a real one, used for a number of years on a range of dedicated word processors. You will see that there are relatively few extra keys, and that most of these are clearly marked with their function. The system in question makes great use of initial letters as 'mnemonics' in its command sequences. W stands for word, P for paragraph, L for line and so on. This makes the system very easy to use. Other systems might have more keys than this, so that instead of using M for move, there might be a special key for the purpose. Other systems might have fewer keys – almost down to the basic QWERTY layout of the central block on the illustration. These would most likely belong to microcomputer systems using word-processing packages. On these, even movements of the cursor have to be controlled by combinations of ordinary keys, so a great many special codes will need to be learned.

Here is a selection of the various keys which you might find on a word processor, with explanations of what they will do. Again, I must emphasise that all systems are different, and manufacturers use different names for similar functions. We can only talk in general terms here, and hope that we cover at least most of the possibilities.

Text entry and editing keys

Command   This is used to begin many of the command sequences. It tells the machine that the next key to be pressed is an instruction, and not text to be displayed on the screen as part of a document.

Control   Some systems – typically the computer-based ones – use CONTROL in much the same way as COMMAND, that is, to alert the system that an instruction is on the way.

Code   This usually changes the function of an individual key – or even the entire keyboard – revealing a 'third keyboard' of special characters, symbols or codes which can be used to give instructions to the printer for line-spacing or pitch changes, sub- and superscript and a host of other uses.

Cursor controls   Where special keys are provided, these are usually marked simply with arrows indicating the direction of movement. On a word processor, these are usually grouped together to one side of the main keyboard. There may also be separate keys for quick cursor movement to the beginning of successive words, lines, sentences or paragraphs; to the beginning or end of the displayed text, or to the limits of the screen. The cursor may be used for shading in areas of text which are to be erased, deleted, moved or otherwise operated upon, or it may be used to indicate the intended location of a particular operation, for example, where a piece of inserted text is to appear. Many of the microcomputer WP packages use a combination of the CONTROL key and the diamond formed by E, S, D and X on the QWERTY keyboard to move the cursor. By combining these with other keys, various quick cursor movements can be achieved very like those on a more dedicated machine. Where a 'graphics' feature permits the drawing of horizontal and vertical lines, it is the four basic cursor keys which are used to draw on the screen.

Carriage return   Only used during text input to end short lines, or introduce lines of blank space, the carriage return key is on many systems also the EXECUTE key which terminates most commands, telling the machine 'Go and do it!' The CODE key on some systems modifies its effect to produce a 'soft' carriage return indicated on the screen by a special symbol. For example, an address block to be typed on one line of the screen, which will format to the correct layout when it is printed.

Backspace   Depending upon the system, this may erase text, leaving written spaces, or delete text, whereby the following characters will close up. It may also act upon the character on which the cursor is placed, or the one *previous* to it.

Erase   This replaces characters with written spaces. It may be used alone for erasing character by character, or as part of a command sequence for erasing blocks of text.

Delete   When used on the screen, characters beyond those being deleted will move backwards to fill in the gap. It may also be used to delete blocks of text, and in conjunction with other keys may also delete files from the disk.

Repeat   Some keys, notably the '*x*', hyphen and underscore are automatically repeat keys on most machines. Where a separate REPEAT key is provided, this will usually convert any other key to a repeat key, including DELETE and ERASE keys.

'Dead' keys   These usually contain accents for European languages. When a dead key is depressed, the appropriate accent appears on the screen, but the cursor does not advance. It is therefore necessary to type the accent first, then the letter to which it refers. Some systems display the accents properly attached to the characters, others align them only when printing out.

Shift   As on an ordinary typewriter, this key causes any other key to operate in upper case. Used with the normal keyboard, this will produce either capital letters or the upper of the characters marked on the keytops. Used in conjunction with CODE, this may produce yet a 'fourth' keyboard of special codes and symbols.

Shift lock   This will usually put the entire keyboard into upper-case, in effect 'holding the shift key down' as indeed it does on manual typewriters. There may also be a capitals 'mode' which will put all alphabetic characters into upper-case, but leave numerals and symbols unaffected.

Tab   This will move the cursor quickly to 'tab stops' set in the ruler or format line, thus enabling a single line to be indented, or text to be typed in columns.

Autotab or indent   When text is entered to this key, every line is indented to the tab stop at which typing commenced, thereby indenting an entire paragraph. Operation of the carriage return key to end a paragraph will usually cancel the effect of this key, and return the cursor to the left margin of the following line.

Decimal tab   To set, or go to special tabs for the purpose of aligning columns of figures around the decimal points. When figures are entered to these tabs, they enter 'calculator-fashion' each displacing previous figures to the left until the decimal point is entered. Some systems will allow decimal tabs to be used also for right-ranging text.

Mode   Used in conjunction with other keys, this tells the system to behave in a certain way until it is told otherwise. MODE UNDERLINE, for example, will underline text as it is typed; MODE HYPHEN will indicate possible hyphenation points, MODE GRAPHIC will allow you to draw lines on the screen, and so on.

Escape   This is usually on microcomputer systems, to cause whatever operation is being asked for to become effective in the position indicated by the cursor.

File   This is often used as a prefix in place of COMMAND to indicate that the instruction is concerned with a file operation.

Open or save   Used to store text on disk. It is usually followed by the text-name and page number or extension which is being given to a new page or document.

Recall   This key is used to recall text from disk to the screen. Operation of this key usually produces a prompt asking for the text or filename of the required file. Some systems will allow you to recall a page or section of text from the disk and insert it into the relevant page. In such cases the function may either be an option offered during the normal 'RECALL' sequence, on may be a different command known as 'GET' or 'INCLUDE'.

Update   Where an existing file has been recalled from disk and edited, and it is now required to re-store this on disk in its amended form, destroying the original version. This is sometimes achieved by simply repeating the SAVE command. When producing a long or complicated document, it is advisable to UPDATE frequently so that, should anything go wrong, it will only be necessary to repeat work from the point of the previous update.

Page   Used to produce an end-of-page marker in document-oriented systems, or to confirm the placing of a page break during repagination by the system.

Next page/previous page   In systems where the name of the document being currently worked upon is displayed on the screen, these keys enable the operator to call up subsequent or previous pages from the disk without needing to key in the text- or file-name each time.

Go to page   Enables the operator to go straight to a particular page in a document-oriented system without scrolling through all the previous pages.

Most of these functions exist where appropriate in all word-processing systems. It is up to the whim of the individual manufacturer, constrained by the power of the system and available software, how many are represented by dedicated keys. Some microcomputers have a number of 'spare' keys which can be programmed by the operator to perform frequently-used functions. This is by no means an exhaustive list, as a visit to any word-processing exhibition will show, but it contains most of the more common function keys.

The screen   The screen displays at various times, and in various combinations:
- an *index* or *directory* of the files available on a disk;
- menus indicating a choice of task or function;
- format information;
- the page or document currently in use.

Index or directory   Depending upon whether the system is page- or document-oriented, the index will contain either text- or file-names with page numbers and possibly additional page references, or file-names with optional extensions indicating the type of file. In some systems it is possible to call up the index in the middle of working on a page, then return to the page. Other systems will lose any text which is on screen when the index is called, so it is necessary to store the page first, before calling the index.

Menus These are in truth 'bills of fare' offering to the operator a choice of the various functions and operations of which the equipment is capable. There are basically two types of operating system for word processors: one kind uses menus, offering a choice from a list of possibilities, the other is 'command-based' and allows the operator to directly instruct the machine without reference to a menu. The menu-driven systems usually have a 'Main menu' which contains a selection of task groups, each referring to a sub-menu containing theindividual tasks. Menu-driven word-processors may have as few as two menus, referring to, say, filing operations and printing operations. Word-processing packages usually have more. *WordStar,* for example, has no less than seven menus. There may also be 'Help' menus which can be called to the screen when required and explain in greater detail the various functions. To select a task from a menu, it is usually only necessary either to key in a single reference character, or position the cursor on the task required.

At the time of writing, pictorial 'menus' are becoming popular, ostensibly aimed at the non-keyboarding executive. In these, pictorial representations of the various tasks are shown on screen, and the operator merely has to touch the picture to invoke the task required. Alternatively, a 'mouse' may be used to control a cursor or pointer on the screen to indicate the required task.

Format information This consists mainly of instructions which will be acted upon by the printer during production of hard copy. Depending on the machine used, this information may be entered into prepared 'fields' or spaces on the display reserved for the purpose, or it may be entered in list form, when each item is preceded by a code which tells the system what it is.

Format information will typically include:

Width of the page   Measured in *characters,* this is the width of the actual paper used for the printed page. Hence, A4 paper will be 80 characters wide if 10-pitch is being used, 96 if 12-pitch. Not all machines require this setting, relying solely upon the margin settings in the ruler line.

Length of page   Measured in single-spaced lines, this again is the length of the actual paper. The machine needs to know this if a sheet-feeder is attached to the printer, to ensure that every page begins printing at the same distance from the top. During repagination, some systems can calculate the number of lines to be fitted onto a page where there are variations in line-spacing within the text. These systems may use the page-length or form-length as it is sometimes called, as a basis for this calculation.

Lines per page   This is the number of *typed* lines on the screen display which will be regarded by the system as a 'page'. It is usually set by the operator to be the same as the number of lines on the printed page but, as we have already seen, there may be variations in spacing which will change the actual number of lines printed. The lines-per-page setting is more concerned with the number of lines which the system will file as a page. On a page-oriented system each page will be filed separately by number. On a document-oriented system the entire document will be filed as a piece, but the pages will be indicated on the display by some form of 'page-break' – often a dotted line right across the page.

Line-spacing   In most cases this is only effective during printing, but some systems will display material in the line-spacing chosen. Single-spacing is the same as on a typewriter – 6 lines to the inch. At the time of writing there has been no serious attempt to decimalise line-spacing or pitch settings.

Pitch   This is the number of characters which will be printed to the inch. The usual choice is 10, 12 or 15 but some machines will give a much wider choice. Printwheels are currently available for 10, 12, 15 and 20 pitch.

Top margin or offset   This is the number of lines the printer will wind up before beginning to print, measured in single-spaced lines.

Left-print offset   On some systems this is the number of characters which the printer will offset from the left before printing. It is in effect a left margin, and is often used as such. Where there are both left print offset *and* a left margin setting, you must remember that the effect may be cumulative when you print out. If you set a left margin of 10, and the system has a 'default' left print offset of, say, 8, the printed document could have a left margin of 18 characters width.

In addition to the usual format information, a system may also require instructions regarding such things as right margin justification, page numbering, and headers and footers to be placed in the same area of the screen.

The ruler or format line   Most systems will have a horizontal scale or equivalent line which approximates to the scale on the paper bail of a typewriter. Some systems have a permanent line at either top or bottom of the screen. Others have a 'ruler line' which is effective from the top of a document, but which can be duplicated with appropriate changes at any point within the text where changes are to be made in margin or tab settings. The ruler line principally contains the margin settings and tab settings. It may also contain a 'hot zone' towards the right margin within which, if a hyphen is typed, word-wrap will immediately occur. Most systems also use the ruler line to indicate the current position of the cursor.

The active page   This is the page which is currently being worked upon, and is residing or partly residing in the main memory of the system. Depending upon whether the system is page- or document-oriented, the active page may consists of a single page of text containing, say, 60 lines, or an entire document containing many such pages. In the latter case, the whole document is not necessarily held in the machine memory, but sections of it are called from the disk as required without further intervention by the operator.

We are now going to look at some of the more common text entry and editing operations, and see how the operator will see these on the screen.

Typing normally   If you are not using a bell zone, you type, in effect, a continuous line, only using carriage return when you start a new paragraph. The settings of the machine take care of the carriage returns at the end of each line, and word-wraparound ensures that only complete words are typed on a line. If the machine 'runs out of space' in the middle of a word, the beginning of that word is automatically transferred to the next line, as Figures 25 and 26 illustrate.

```
Word-wraparound is what happens when the end of a line of
the chosen length happens to fall in the middle of a word.
When the right hand margin is reached, the machine transf
```

Fig 25   Word-wraparound – before

```
Word-wraparound is what happens when the end of a line of
the chosen length happens to fall in the middle of a word.
When the right-hand margin is reached, the machine
transfers the beginning of the word to the next line.
```

Fig 26   Word-wraparound – after

As there is no need to wait for the carriage to return at the end of each line, your overall typing speed will increase considerably, partly because of the time saved, and also because the rhythm of your typing is unimpaired.

Word wraparound – or word-wrap as it is sometimes called – will also take place after corrections which involve inserting or deleting text. Most systems will reformat the text automatically after such revision, and word-wrap will occur as part of this operation. Some systems however do not reformat automatically, and this has to be done by means of a separate command when the editing has been completed.

When you have completed typing a page, proof-read it from the screen, and make any necessary corrections *before* printing.

Correcting
mis-typed
characters   Most systems will allow you to correct simply by overtyping with the correct character. Some however require you first to erase or delete the mis-keyed character before you can type in the new one.

Here are some of the more common corrections or alterations you will need to make, either on your own initiative or as requested by an originator.

Delete   When you delete text, it is as if it had never been typed. The deleted text disappears, and the remainder of the text closes up to fill in the space.

```
If you wish to delete a word word for any reason you key in
the following sequence
```

Fig 27   Delete – before

To delete a whole word, first position the cursor below the first character of the word and then key in the command required.

```
If you wish to delete a word for any reason you key in the
following sequence.
```

Fig 28   Delete – after

The whole word then disappears and, because it is replaced with 'blank space' and not 'written space', word-wraparound takes place and the remainder of the text closes up.

Erasing text   The important difference between *delete* and *erase* is that erasing replaces the characters with *written* spaces instead of blank space, so the text will not close up as it does after a deletion. Variations on the erase sequence may allow underlining to be removed without erasing the underline characters, and erasing 'graphics' characters without affecting the text and vice versa.

Defining a text quantity   To erase, delete, move or otherwise edit a quantity of text, you will often need to *define* it, so that the system knows which area is involved. You may define text as a linear amount such as word, line, sentence or paragraph, or as a rectangular area of the screen. Text thus defined may be highlighted on the screen by a number of methods. Some systems will produce a half-tone shading over the affected characters, others will 'reverse out' displaying the characters as 'negatives' of their usual form. Others are able to vary the brightness of selected characters on the display. The more basic WP packages will not highlight text, but it will need to be defined by codes typed at the beginning and end of the passages to be affected.

```
You can define a quantity of text as consisting of a single
word or you can if you wish define it as a complete line.

You can also define a whole paragraph if you want to.
Whichever you choose, the characters thus defined will be
covered in a green half-tone effect. This allows you to see
exactly what you have defined, while still being able to
read it.
```

Fig 29   A quantity, defined and highlighted

Defining a screen area   You may sometimes need to define, not a specific quantity of text such as a sentence, but a rectangular area of the screen, whatever it contains. This may be in order to retain the format of the affected text, or, in the case of graphics or figure work it may be that the characters cannot be defined as a text quantity. The area so defined is variously described by different systems as a 'table', a 'column' or a 'block'. It may be defined by drawing in a highlight with the cursor, or by placing markers at the beginning of the top line and the end of the bottom line.

If you wish to define a quantity of text as a table, it must
be rectangular in shape.

Any spaces within the rectangle are automatically filled
with written spaces, which behave like characters.

Fig 30   Defining a table or column

Care must be taken when moving text which has been defined as a rectangular
area. Whereas text defined as a linear quantity will usually *insert* into a new
position, a table or column may *overwrite* existing text under certain circumstances.

Inserting   To insert text you may only need to position the cursor where the insertion is to
begin, and then type the new text. In this case the new text 'elbows' the old out of
the way as it goes. One problem with this method is that it is easy to delete
characters accidentally from the 'following' text. To avoid this, operators will
often insert a number of carriage returns to provide an area of blank space after
the inserted text. Mistakes in deletion will simply delete the 'spare' carriage
returns, and any remaining when the inserted material has been typed can easily
be deleted to close up the text.

Other systems, as Figures 31-34 show, drop the text following the point of
insertion down by one line to give a blank space into which the insertion is typed.
Typing beyond the end of the blank line simply causes the text to drop down
again, and so on until the command is cancelled. The following text will then
close up and word-wrap will occur.

In this example we wish to a word which has been inadvertently
omitted by the typist. In ordinary typewriting this almost
always means a complete re-type.

Fig 31   Inserting – before

All the text beyond the cursor falls away by one line.

In this example we wish to
                          a word which has been inadvertently
omitted by the typist. In ordinary typewriting this almost
always means a complete retype.

Fig 32   Inserting – the text drops away

The insert material is then typed in:

In this example we wish to insert
                          a word which has been inadvertently
omitted by the typist. In ordinary typewriting this almost
always means a complete re-type.

Fig 33   Inserting – the new text is typed in

The command is terminated upon which the remaining text closes up to follow on from the insertion (word wraparound).

In this example we wish to insert a word which has been inadvertently omitted by the typist. In ordinary typewriting this almost always means a complete re-type.

Fig 34 Inserting – the text closes up

On some systems, word-wrap does not automatically occur when the insert command is terminated, but needs to be effected by an additional command.

Centring Centring text is easy on most word processors. On some, the text to be centred is preceded by a coded character, and the line is centred when the operator keys carriage return. On others the whole of the text to be centred is typed in fully-blocked style, and centred afterwards either line by line, or as a single operation.

—

T H E   B E L L   H O T E L

WORCESTER

SATURDAY, 17th August, 1979

LUNCHEON

Tomato Soup
or
Grapefruit

* * *

Fried Fillet of Plaice - Sauce Tartare
Roast Chicken, Sausage and Stuffing
Bread Sauce
Roast and Creamed Potatoes
Spring Cabbage
Garden Peas

* * *

Peach Melba
Fruit Tart with Custard
or
Cheese and Biscuits

* * *

Coffee

* * *

Fig 35 Centring – before

THE BELL HOTEL

WORCESTER

SATURDAY, 17th August, 1979

LUNCHEON

Tomato Soup
or
Grapefruit

* * *

Fried Fillet of Plaice - Sauce Tartare
Roast Chicken, Sausage and Stuffing
Bread Sauce
Roast and Creamed Potatoes
Spring Cabbage
Garden Peas

* * *

Peach Melba
Fruit Tart with Custard
or
Cheese and Biscuits

* * *

Coffee

* * *

Fig 36 Centring – after

Centring is normally carried out between margins. You may however be able to centre text around the cursor position, around a specified character position or column number, or within a defined area of screen such as a 'table'. This last is particularly useful where a system has a graphics facility, and it may be necessary to centre text within 'boxes', such as in an organisation chart.

When typing work which is to be centred, it is important to end each line with a carriage return. Failure to do this may result in the centred text being reformatted during subsequent text-editing.

Reformatting   Most word processors will allow existing text to be reformatted to new margins, either as a whole page or as defined sections within a document. Some systems require this to be done by setting an entire new ruler line at the point where the reformatting is to commence. Text after this point will then obey the new formats until another ruler line is encountered.

Other systems will allow the operator to reformat sections of text such as paragraphs so as to indent them from left, right or both margins. If this is done, a temporary right margin is usually indicated on the screen. Subsequent editing of the indented paragraph will take place within the indented margins, and will not result in the text reverting to the original left margin.

Printing such indented text with a 'justify' option will also ensure that the temporary right margin is justified as well as the main right margin. Remember that when you indent a paragraph from both margins, it still contains the same amount of text. If the paragraph is narrower, the lines will not hold the same number of characters, so extra lines will be created to hold the displaced text. This can create problems if you already have the maximum number of lines allowed by the lines-per-page setting in the page description.

Copying   Your word processor may allow you to copy text from one location to another. This facility can be used either to duplicate items which occur a number of times on a page, or to move text from one place to another. In the first instance the original text would remain in its original position as well as appearing in the new position, and in the second it would be deleted once the copy had been safely installed in its new position. This feature uses a section of the main memory called a 'buffer' or 'putaside memory', which stores the amount of text to be moved or copied for as long as is necessary to transfer it to a new location.

Depending on the system used, there may be separate command sequences for COPY and MOVE or it may need to be defined as a word, line, sentence, paragraph or table, or it may be isolated by inserting 'markers' at the beginning and end. The new position is usually indicated by placing the cursor at the point where the insertion is to begin.

Moving   The more advanced systems will allow you to move text on the screen by 'walking' it to a new position. The text is first defined as a number of complete lines of text or as a rectangular block. Fine adjustment may be possible using the cursor to shade in additional areas, or to remove parts of the shaded area. The defined area can then be moved on the screen, by using the cursor controls.

Depending upon the limitations of the particular system in use, you may be able to move lines of text vertically, columns of figures horizontally, and rectangular 'tables' in any direction. This feature is particularly useful when doing complicated display work or using the graphics facility to draw charts and diagrams.

Merging   Most word processors will allow text from different files to be merged during printing to produce such things as personalised standard letters, forms, and documents built up from standard paragraphs. The actual methods used – of which there are a number – are beyond the scope of this book. For this, and other more advanced features of word processors and similar computer-based equipment including the basics of communication between machines, I will refer you to the companion volume *Beyond Word Processing* from the same publisher.

For the moment, and because we are on the subject of the screen, note that you may be able to call up a sample page of a merged document to the screen in order to check that the merge has been correctly set up.

This then is as far as this book will take you in general terms of text entry and editing. Readers wishing to know more should refer either to the machine-specific literature supplied for their own machine, or to the aforementioned companion book. Having proceeded so far, particularly if your reading has been supplemented by hands-on experience of at least one type of equipment, you should by now have a fair idea of what a word processor can do for you.

6 Who can use one?

Potential users of word processors

Having now digested quite a lot of information about the hardware, what the equipment consists of, what it does and how it does it, let us now turn to the most important part of the word-processing system – the people who are going to benefit from its use. What kind of a business is going to use this new generation of office aids? It is a common fallacy that only big business can gain from the use of sophisticated equipment. The need for word processors depends on the kind of work which is to be done – not on the size of organisation.

Creative writers I myself, for example, have found a word processor invaluable while writing this book. A great deal of laborious retyping and correcting has been avoided, or at least made much easier by being able to proof-read, edit and amend each page on screen before committing it to paper. As this applies to me, so it would apply to anyone carrying out any form of creative writing whether it be advertising copy, technical reports, or a Government paper on the economic situation.

Solicitors There are certain classifications of potential users of word processors which are so obvious that they immediately spring to the minds of most people. Solicitors, for example, whose output in tangible form consists in the main of lengthy documents written in archaic terminology. Most of these can be reduced to a number of standard formats which, when required can be brought to the screen, personalised by addition of the particulars of the parties concerned, and printed out at high speed. The advantage, as with all word-processor work, is that only the keyed-in additions would need to be checked. The bulk of the document, be it Last Will & Testament, Contract or Conveyance, once committed to the machine's memory, would be reproduced time and time again, entirely without error. Much of the correspondence of a solicitor is of a stereotyped nature, consisting of requests for information from other solicitors, or replies to such requests. This also can be dealt with more speedily by the use of word-processing, as can the normal day-to-day one-off type of letter.

Insurance The work of the Insurance Company, by its very nature, also consists largely of standard letters and documents of a repetitive nature. Reminders of premiums due, if not already sent out by computer, can be called up from the file, and by use of the 'Sort & Merge' feature prepared automatically.

Engineering Engineering companies, in particular those engaged in the manufacture of high-value capital equipment, spend a great deal of time compiling technical specifications and quotations, many of which differ only in detail. Spare-parts lists frequently have to be brought up to date because of changes in numbers or availability of certain items. Again it must be stressed that in such a case, *only the alterations need to be checked* not the entire list, as would be the case with a normal retype. Maintenance schedules, Service Contract reminders and mailing lists of existing or prospective customers are also applications within the service divisions of engineering companies.

Motor industry The motor industry, including its service side, would have its own uses for word processing. It too has a vast number of parts lists, price lists, stock availability lists, standard forms of correspondence with customers and third-party suppliers, service manuals, work schedules, inspection reports and so on. By keeping customer records on disk, the selective merging facility of most systems can be used to send out reminders of services due, information about new models or special deals.

Estate agents The estate agent who receives an enquiry from a prospective house-buyer can instantly call to the screen of a word-processor a list of properties in a selected area, with, for example, three or more bedrooms and gas central-heating. Alternatively, he can ask for a list of all properties of a certain value, and a copy would be printed within seconds if required. If he also happens to be an Auctioneer and Surveyor, as many estate agents are, he will find uses for word processing in preparing surveyors' reports, auction sale catalogues, and mailing lists of selected categories of clients likely to be interested in a particular sale.

Local authorities Local authorities, consisting as they do of representatives of many trades and professions, must be among the largest potential users of word processing. In addition to the requirements in common with those in private practice among the solicitors, architects and surveyors, accountants and other professional bodies, there are those needs peculiar to the public service sector. Electoral registers are in constant need of revision; Standing Orders, Committee and Council Minutes, Housing Lists, circular letters of many kinds, invitations to tender, are only a few of the thousand and one jobs for the word processor in even the smallest local authority. In the course of the administration of justice, a great deal of paper is generated by the Courts and the police force. Much of this is of a repetitive nature, and could be profitably entrusted to the word processor.

Agencies Airlines, travel agents and theatre booking agencies are already making use of on-line computers to acquire an up-to-the-minute knowledge of the availability of accommodation, whether it be in the form of a seat in an aircraft or a theatre, or a villa in some Mediterranean resort. Employment agencies are interested in word processors on a number of fronts. Not only has the demand for trained operators opened up lucrative new markets for their clients, but many are now diversifying into a training activity, or providing 'WP Temps' able to turn their hands to a variety of different makes of equipment. In their own offices the word processor is ideal for maintaining records of both clients and job-seekers; constructing job-specifications, drawing up questionnaires, providing professional-looking CVs and many other jobs.

Banking Banks have now almost completely computerised the day-to-day handling of customers' accounts, but an enormous amount of work goes on behind the scenes in administration, investment services, foreign business and general matters.

General Apart from these specific applications to individual professional or business groups, there are many general-purpose uses which may apply to virtually any business or community organisation. Personnel records stored in the files of word processor can be called up if it is necessary for any reason to select a list of people with particular qualifications or aptitudes. Mailing lists can be made highly selective to include only prospects living in a certain area, or in a house of a certain type or within a specified range of values, or the owners of a particular make or model of car, or known to have certain interests or hobbies – the possibilities are endless. Personalised sales-letters, each one produced as a top copy, are much more likely to be read and to achieve results than the printed circular or the obviously duplicated letter with a name and address typed in – probably in non-matching type.

Handouts for the firm's open day, programmes of sporting events, even the canteen menu can be produced on a word processor. The marketing department is able, particularly if the word processor has a graphics function, to produce bar-charts, graphs and tables for use as handouts or visual aids at sales presentations. The Training Manager will make good use of it to create imaginative training aids in the form of overhead projector transparencies, notes and handouts for training sessions, and to keep his records of personnel undergoing training up to date.

The ability to change typefaces and pitch at will allows a freedom of typographical design impossible with the ordinary typewriter, and the facility of right-hand margin justification and multi-margin settings enable copy of almost print standard to be achieved. For work which must be printed for the sake of appearance, great savings can be made in preparing work for the printer. There are now a number of typesetting agencies which will accept customers' copy on disk. This saves the considerable cost of re-keying, at the same time shifting some of the responsibility for proof-reading and correctness of copy to the originator. Instruction manuals, training manuals, salesmen's manuals, all take on a new professional appearance, and in so doing enhance the company image.

There is even benefit for the company or authority whose executives hold office in extra-mural organisations. The circular letter to the members of a local operatic society or tennis club which used to take up a full morning of the Managing Director's secretary's time is now whizzed off in a few minutes – with a consequent saving to the company.

Education   The educational sector (universities, colleges of further and higher education and schools) will all benefit by possession of, or access to, a word processor. As well as the all-important task of training the executive and operator in the use and application of word processing, there are many tasks connected with teaching which could perhaps be undertaken by the students themselves in certain circumstances. The prospectus, for example, needs updating each year. Time-tabling is a job which could be helped by the ability to pull out from store lists of students opting for certain subjects; Speech-day programmes, class-lists, exam lists, stock-lists and requisitions, students' records, a list of students with certain qualifications or aspirations for prospective employers, class-notes, handouts, OHP transparencies – the list goes on and on.

Small businesses

The large public-service organisations and nationalised industries such as the National Coal Board, gas, electricity and water undertakings have all been aware for some time of the benefits of word processing, and for some time have been leading the way in the use of this kind of equipment. Larger businesses and professional practices have also been quick to realise the savings possible through increasing productivity. It is the smaller businesses that do not yet seem to have realised that considerable savings can be made. The cost-effectiveness of labour in the small business or private practice is usually much higher in proportion than in the huge corporation. There is less duplication of effort and function, less administration and supervision. The savings achievable by an increase in efficiency are therefore likely to be greater in effect than they would be in a larger firm. We are all familiar with the situation in the small business where senior executives and secretarial staff are often discovered carrying out quite menial tasks simply because there is nobody else available at the time. How many of us have walked into one of these small firms and asked the individual operating the duplicator if the boss is around, only to receive the rejoinder, 'I *am* the boss – what can I do for you?' The reason that the boss is working the duplicator is possibly something like this. A special letter has to go out that night, and while the office-junior is laboriously ploughing through lists of customers to find those in a particular category, who could perhaps use a particular type of machine or service, and then typing out the envelopes, the boss's secretary is hammering out for the third time a long involved report in which a few essential changes have had to be made: all jobs which could have been tackled quite easily – and much more quickly – by word processing. This is the kind of situation that arises all too often in the small business. How often do we find the wholesaler having to retype an entire stock-list or price-list in order to accommodate a few changes made by a manufacturer? Or the small-practice solicitor whose private secretary spends most of her time typing out one-off copies of Contracts and Conveyances or similar legal documents?

More than one job at once

The cry all too often heard in the small office (and in many big ones too) is 'I've only one pair of hands!' This truism does not, however, necessarily mean that only one job can be done at a time. Some of the operations of which a word processor is capable may be carried out 'in background', that is to say while not occupying the keyboard or screen of the processor. Printing, for instance is one such task. While a lengthy document is being printed-out, at several times the speed at which the most accomplished typist could operate, the main memory of the CPU is free for the operator to use to prepare the next job. Alternatively, many of the 'Locate' or 'String-search' functions can be carried out independently of the operator, thereby allowing her to do other work, either on or away from the word processor.

All this is just the tip of a very large iceberg. It is impossible to list every possible application of word processing under all possible circumstances. It is equally difficult for an outside consultant to assess the total value to a company of a word processor. He *may* know everything of which the word processor is capable, but he certainly will not know enough about the inner workings of the company to be able to pinpoint every possible application for word processing in that company's organisation. The outside consultant, or manufacturer's representative who can do this has not yet been born. This is the kind of thing which can only be discovered from *inside* the company, by the firm's own 'Organisation and Methods' team or management consultants or, most likely, by the bright girl who sits behind the keyboard of the processor and who has, more than anybody else, a more intimate knowledge of what she – and it – can do. She is also often in a position to see the shortcomings of the company's administration system. It is she who can often say to the boss, 'Why don't we do such and such on the word processor?' Or perhaps, 'If we changed the design of the form that we send out to job-applicants, we could keep the whole of our personnel records on disk'.

This is where the superiority of the human brain over all forms of automation comes to the fore. It also brings the realisation that the better the brain behind the keyboard, the more effective is going to be the introduction of word processing, and the greater the value to be extracted from it.

This then, is perhaps an appropriate point at which to look at the kind of people who will operate a word procesing system.

7 Who will operate it?

Importance of people

We now come to the most important part of a word processing system – people. No matter how advanced the technology, we are still reliant upon the skill of human beings to make it work. The success or failure of a system depends entirely upon the people who will operate it. Note that I said 'people' and not 'person', because a word processor does not only involve a girl sitting at a keyboard. The originator also plays an important part. The time will come when all an executive has to do is to pick up a microphone and dictate into it, and the machine will produce perfectly-typed, beautifully set-out hard copy directly from his dictation. When it does – unless standards of dictation are very different from what we experience today – some extremely peculiar letters will result.

Word input   In preparation for that day, or to make the best of what technology we already have, let us consider what is required of the originator. In Chapter 2 we looked at the various methods of providing an input to a word processing system. You will remember that they fell into four main types: longhand draft, shorthand dictation, the dictation machine, and direct keyboarding by the executive.

Longhand draft   If longhand draft is the only way, and we must accept that there are occasions when this is so, then we should insist upon legibility, and total unambiguity of instructions. There should in theory be few instances when it is necessary to reprocess material originally produced from longhand draft. One assumes that the reason for its being produced in this way is because it is the kind of document which requires careful thought and consideration of grammatical construction. This may be either for the sake of clarity, or in order to produce the maximum effect – as in the case of publicity materials, sales letters, advertisements and so on. Having given so much thought to the content, provided that the two criteria of legibility and clarity of instruction are observed, there should be little reason for the document not coming out right the first time. The submission of longhand drafts which could, and should, have been dictated, should be resisted, militantly if necessary, by either relegating them to the bottom of the priority list, or returning them to the originator with a polite request that they be dictated.

Shorthand dictation   Shorthand dictation, as we discussed in Chapter 2, is far from being the ideal form of input to a word processing system, as it necessitates the operator being away from the keyboard for long periods of time. Take an hour's typical shorthand-taking session and compare this with the amount of work which *could* have been done on the word processor during that time. You will see that insistence upon shorthand as a means of input can decimate the potential productivity of the operator, and of course of the machine.

An exception may be made in the case of the Secretary/Personal Assistant, where dictation as such consists mostly of notes. The secretary herself is required to compose replies to correspondence in accordance with brief instructions from her boss. The instructions may well be taken down in shorthand.

Dictation machines There is absolutely no doubt that dictation into a machine or centralised dictation system is by far the most efficient means of providing input to a word processor. It has never been difficult to prove the economics of machine dictation as opposed to shorthand, even using conventional methods of producing the final copy on an ordinary typewriter. As a result of the massive increase in the productivity of the typist brought about by word processors, the gap has widened even further. The weak link in the chain is, and always has been, the inability of the executive to dictate clearly, concisely and in the correct order, the material he wishes to be typed.

Dictator-training The first consideration then should be the training, or retraining of the dictators to an acceptable level. Those forward-thinking companies or authorities which have already endeavoured to provide some form of training for established dictators will be aware of the problems to be encountered. It is difficult to persuade an executive who has perhaps been dictating correspondence for a number of years, either into a machine or to a secretary, that he is in need of training. 'Any fool can dictate,' he will say, and of course he is quite right – and many do so, as you may gather from talking to any group of practising secretaries. Regrettably, the bad habits of a lifetime of untrained dictation may cause the typist to waste a great deal of time either retyping badly dictated matter, or listening through entire tapes in order to extract the general gist of the matter before daring to commit anything to paper.

The best time to introduce some element of dictator-training is at the moment of introducing a new dictation system. Tuition in the art of dictation can be disguised as instruction in the use of the new equipment. At other times it may prove difficult to instruct established dictators. It usually works out that the worst offenders, who are in the greatest need of instruction, are those who by devious means avoid taking the course. Providing that some form of directive can be issued, in-house dictator training can be very useful indeed. It can be administered by the company's own training department, by outside consultants who specialise in this kind of work, or perhaps in conjunction with the local colleges of further education. Most of these will be only too happy to assist provided that there is sufficient demand. Bearing in mind the problems associated with the training of *established* dictators, and in order to prevent perpetuating the situation as it now stands, it would seem that the most sensible time to introduce training in the art of dictation would be during a person's business education. At this stage it is usually apparent by the nature of the course that the student aspires to executive status. As such, it is likely that at some stage of his career he is going to be required to dictate into a dictation machine. He (or she) is amenable to learning at this time, and will readily accept that a degree of training *is* necessary in this small but important part of business life. Most Business Studies courses these days include an element of Communication, and what is dictation if it is not communication between the originator and the typist? It raises some interesting possibilities for cross-modular assignments, and introduces the possibility of co-operation between Business Studies and

Secretarial groups. The efforts of the dictators may be transcribed for them by the secretarial students, both gaining valuable experience in the process. The dictator will see the results of his errors, and will no doubt be told forthrightly of his shortcomings. The student typists will benefit from practice in transcribing far-from-perfect dictation – the kind of dictation in fact which they are likely to encounter in real life. This is usually far removed from the beautifully modulated tones on the tapes produced for them by their teachers. It has even been suggested that all potential dictators should be required at some point during their training to transcribe from their own, or somebody else's dictation. They would then better appreciate the problems faced by the audio-typist in working from recorded dictation. The outline of a short course for dictators is included in *Beyond Word Processing*, the companion volume to this book.

A short course in dictation might consist of basic instruction in the use of the dictation machine and correct handling of the microphone, followed by an easy exercise in dictation of a piece of prepared copy. This would be transcribed and eventually returned to the student for comparison with the original. The same piece of dictation, but this time including the correct conventions and instructions to the typist could then be given out. This would then be dictated and transcribed, and the differences between the result and the original attempt duly noted. The students could then be led through a series of exercises introducing the use of punctuation of various kinds: figures; the need to spell out difficult names of people or places; the use of the phonetic alphabet; the need to spell out homophones or technical or professional terms; the avoidance of the more common dictation faults – pipe-sucking, paper-rustling, mumbling and so on. Having mastered the basic principles, the students could then be required to compose suitable replies to given documents. It is here that the science of precise communication, business letter-writing, formulation of reports and memos could be incorporated as set out by the various examining bodies. Such basic training, which need not take up a great deal of time, would bring to an end most of the problems which are today associated with the use of audio systems. It would also of course add to the efficiency of a word processor.

Direct keyboarding
Returning to our four methods of input, it is likely that, with the probable appearance of personal computers or computer terminals on the desks of many executives, a certain amount of keyboarding skill will need to be introduced at this level. This is not to say that all executives should be capable of typing at 25 wpm or more, though some may wish to proceed to this level. Typewriting as a personal skill would be a useful attribute to many in both business and private life. It may well be that keyboarding skills will become a recognised part of the curriculum for *all* above a certain scholastic ability in further education, or even in the secondary or upper schools.

For those executives who are prepared – or even eager – to input their own text, or to edit first drafts which have been keyed-in for them, machines are becoming ever more user-friendly. The originator who is content to 'hunt and peck' around the keyboard now finds that there are ways of controlling the machine other than keying-in a series of codes and commands. The 'mouse' a simple hand-held device which can be trundled around the desk-top controls cursor movement, and can be used to select tasks. 'Touch-screen' techniques enable even the most ham-fisted originator to point to the function required on a pictorial menu on the screen. Software – particularly for the popular personal computers – is becoming more sophisticated almost by the hour! Spectacular graphics effects, varying typefaces, superb displayed work, can all be turned out by virtually untrained executives. Voice-input is only a matter of time – but here we return to the ability of the originator to dictate clearly and concisely.

Principles of word processing Remaining with the executives for the moment, it is essential that they, as well as the potential operators of word-processing systems, are aware of the basic principles governing the use of such equipment. Without such knowledge, it will be impossible for the potential purchaser or user of a word processor to appreciate fully the benefits which may be obtained from its use. It may also lead to the purchase of a great deal of unsuitable equipment. A salesman cannot be blamed for trying to sell the more expensive of his range of equipment, and it may well be that many word processors are purchased and sadly under-used. This could be for two reasons: either the application was for a less advanced machine in the first place, or the user does not realise all that is possible with the machine which he has purchased.

If the right system is to be obtained, and the fullest possible use made of it, the purchaser and his advisers must know in advance what they are looking for in terms of capacity and features. Conversely, many prospective users of word processing may rush out and buy cheap microcomputers with bolt-on peripherals and cheap printers. They will then complain bitterly because they do not have the performance of the properly constructed system. It is as vital to know the limitations, for example, of the tape cassette as against the floppy disk, as it is to appreciate the capabilities of each type of processor.

Word output

Let us turn now to the people who will actually operate the word processors.

Qualifications So far as actual keyboarding skill is concerned, there is likely to be little difference between the word processor and the fast, accurate, top-copy typist who performs on an ordinary electronic typewriter. For the most part, as we have seen in Chapter 5, the keyboard consists of the standard QWERTY layout which every typist is trained to use. The only additions are the special function and command keys which are peculiar to each make of machine. For this reason it will not be possible, or even desirable, for colleges of further education to turn out fully-fledged word-processor operators. The student who will be likely to succeed as a word-processor operator will probably leave college with typewriting, audio-typing, perhaps a reasonable competence in shorthand or a note-taking system, and a knowledge of the basic principles of word processing. From this point it will be the responsibility of the machine manufacturers, or the employers' own training resources, to complete training on the particular machine to be used.

TRAINING NEEDS
IN
SECRETARIAL STUDIES
(WP OPERATORS)

1 TYPEWRITING
2 AUDIO-TYPING
3 LANGUAGE SKILLS (SPG)
4 NOTE-TAKING SHORTHAND
5 PROOF-READING
6 WP PRINCIPLES

SPG? – Spelling, Punctuation and Grammar! The ability to sort out imperfect syntax, spell from dictated material *without* the aid of a spelling-check program, and punctuate unequivocably is paramount. When the day dawns that direct voice-input does become a commercially-viable option, one shudders to think what some of the results will look like. It will be largely up to the WP operator to sort it all out and reduce the ramblings of the originator to crisp prose.

Personality In addition to the language and motor skills already mentioned, certain personality traits will point towards probable success as a word-processor operator. The good candidate will have an analytical mind, and the ability to 'think on her feet'. Many jobs can be tackled in different ways, and it will be up to the bright operator to spot the quickest and easiest method. She will be 'unflappable' and not prone to panic if the machine does the unexpected. She will be 'happy with machines' and in this respect the good audio-typist is one of the most likely subjects for conversion, as she already accepts machinery as part of her life. The girl who panics if her headset plug falls out; or who is all thumbs in the practice office; or who can only do things 'by the book' would do well to look elsewhere.

PERSONAL ATTRIBUTES
OF A
WP OPERATOR

1 HAPPY WITH MACHINES
2 UNFLAPPABLE
3 THINKS ON HER FEET
4 LOGICAL
5 PROBABLY GOOD AT SCRABBLE

Why Scrabble? Because, like Scrabble, the word processor will always present a number of alternatives. The successful Scrabble player does not stick down the first word that leaps out from the seven tiles. Rather he or she stops to consider the possible alternatives, and whether better advantage can be gained by using the tiles in a different way. Similarly the good WP operator will always be on the lookout for quicker, easier or more effective ways of doing her job.

Since the first edition of this book in 1980, a lot has been written about job opportunities in word processing and the electronic office in general. Among those looking at this field has been the Manpower Services Commission, which set up a working party to lay down specimen job profiles and training recommendations. The findings of this working party (on which I had the pleasure of serving) are published by the MSC in a booklet – one of a series of three on Text Processing – called *Job Profiles and Training Recommendations for Operators and Supervisors*.

The booklet sets out skills requirements for four grades of WP operator plus an MP supervisor. In a Competence Tble, under the headings of the five jobs described, are listed the degrees of competence required in a number of machine skills, language skills, allied knowledge of office procedures etc., personal abilities and, where applicable, training and supervisory skills. There is also a career ladder showing likely points of entry and progression through the various grades of operator. I can do no better than to recommend the reader to obtain a copy of this booklet and see in greater detail the requirements for jobs in word processing.

So far as job-opportunities are concerned, information technology, of which word processing is a fundamental constituent, is *the* emergent skills area at the present time. All types and sizes of business from the one-man set-up to the multinational giants are investing in information technology in a big way. There is no scarcity of job-opportunities for the skilled operator who is adaptable and prepared to move with the time and the technology.

To the young person eager to find employment involving the use of exciting new high-technology equipment, the advice is somewhat hackneyed, but as true as it ever was. Concentrate on laying down a solid foundation of office skills and associated knowledge. It is like painting a house – most of the work is done at the preparation stage, cleaning down and making good the surfaces for the final glossy coat of paint. A good solid grounding in typing, language skills and office practice with appropriate certificates gained is worth far more than a superficial knowledge of operating one out of hundreds of word processors. As any decorator will tell you, work done in the preparation shows in the finished job. It is the same in office technology – the final gloss of machine-specific training on the equipment which you are going to use is easily attained in a week or so on a manufacturer's training course. Use the time which you have in full-time or further education to prepare the grounding for that final gloss!

As you will see if you read the MSC booklet, jobs can range from low-grade clerk-type activities involving form-filling, standard letters and similar routine work needing a bare minimum of knowledge in excess of basic typing, to highly-skilled creative activities stretching to the full both machine and operator. The average operator will probably have intermediate qualifications in secretarial studies. She will be expected to tackle a wide variety of jobs from written draft, audio-dictation and possibly shorthand though this is by no means the essential skill that it was. She will need to be flexible in attitude, not only in regard to meeting work-flow demands, but also in adapting to new technology as it emerges. Finally, she will be able to communicate clearly with others, both to understand what is required of her, and possibly to pass on instruction to juniors. Secretaries too, will find more use for word processors, using the machines to cope more easily and quickly with routine tasks, thereby freeing themselves for more useful and creative involvement in their managers' activities.

Work environment

Having looked at the *kind* of jobs which are available to the word-processor operator, let us now consider the types of environment in which she could find herself doing them. With the hiving-off of all the jobs which *cannot* be done on a word processor, it is inevitable that some degree of centralisation will result.

Work groups The word-processor secretary may find herself to be part of a work group, consisting of a small number of managers and their necessary support staff. The composition of the group will be determined by the job-content of the managers *not*, as was so often the case in the past, by the *status* of the managers. There is no room for class-consciousness in the modern office! The work-content of the group may be such that it consists mainly of administrative tasks, and has little output in the form of hard copy. In such a case there will only be a requirement for perhaps one or two word-processor secretaries, with a larger complement of administrative support staff: filing clerks, accounts clerks, personal assistants and the like.

The work of the group may, on the other hand, result in a large amount of correspondence or hard copy in the form of legal documents, minutes, reports or involved quotations, but with little non-typing work. Then, the word processor operators – clerks and secretaries – will be in the majority. A work-group can be as large or small as the number of managers and their job-content demands. This concept will be preferred by people who like working in close co-operation with a limited number of colleagues. There will be opportunities for specialisation within their particular area, movement between the functions of word processing and administration inside the group, and the likelihood of progression towards management as the ultimate goal.

Semi-centralisation At one stage removed from small self-contained groups, the nature of a company's business may lend itself better to centralisation of one or other of the functions of word processing or administration. So far as the word processor operator is concerned this could lead to one of two situations. The administrative, or non-typing function may be centralised in, shall we say, an accounts centre, or sales office. The word-processor secretary will be decentralised and, as with the work-group, will be responsible to a small number of managers for whom she will perform all the necessary typing tasks.

Alternatively the nature of business may be such that it is the word-processing function which is centralised, with administrative assistants shared by small groups of managers. In this case the word-processor operator, whether clerk or secretary, will be based in a centre where all typing tasks are carried out for the whole organisation.

Within the centre there is a clearly-defined career-ladder up to the level of supervisor, and experience will be gained in a number of varied tasks. This is probably the setting for the individual who likes working among a lot of people, enjoys variety in her work, sees no particular need for personal contact with the managers, and has no aspirations towards management.

Full centralisation The ultimate in centralisation exists where *all* common services of typing, word processing, administrative support, reprographics and post-room are gathered together as a total support-group for the entire management. Each separate function will work under its own Section-Head, who will be under the direction of either a Word-processor Supervisor, or an Administration Supervisor. These in turn will be responsible to a Centre Supervisor, or Office Manager, who will report directly to management at a high level.

Similar opportunities for advancement will exist within the centre to those where only one function is centralised. Movement between sections will be much easier however, and indeed will most likely to be encouraged. For the word-processor operator who wishes to acquire wide experience over a great variety of tasks, who likes working in busy surroundings where there is always something happening, and who wants to see a clearly-defined path of promotion ahead, this is the place. Whether the idea is to gain experience rapidly in order to move on to better things, or work steadily through the system until she arrives at her goal of supervisory status, the big centre in the large company or authority is the best place for her. If on the other hand she hates crowds, likes to be left alone to do her own thing, and prefers to work for one, or a small number of bosses, she will not be happy in this kind of situation and would be better to look elsewhere for employment.

. . . but in real life . . . don't expect to find everything as clear-cut as it seems to be in these few illustrations! These are models – copy-book cases which look good on the Organisation Chart, and are beloved of Organisation and Methods teams, or Management Consultants. In practice, you are quite likely to find a hotch-potch of the various systems merging, overlapping, or coexisting within the same organisation. This is because what may be ideal for the Sales and Marketing Division is no use at all to the Production Division – and the Directors insist on having their own secretaries anyhow – and Personnel couldn't *possibly* allow any of their work into the Centre because of its confidential nature – and all the other reasons why everybody thinks that *their* job is different from everybody else's!

The main thing is that *every* Division, each in its own way, needs word processing for *something*. That's where you come in.

8 Where do we go from here?

From word processors to integrated office systems

Having completely revised this book, originally written at the end of the 1970s and published in 1980, it seems incredible that in such a fast-moving area as word processing so much that was written at that time is still valid. What has happened of course, is that the basic *principles* which are what we are concerned with have not changed a great deal. Nor, I think, are they likely to in the foreseeable future.

What *has* changed, and is likely to continue to change at an accelerating rate, is the means of *achieving* the basic principles. Hardware – the machines and attachments which can be seen, handled and used – has become smaller and cheaper. Particularly in the field of printers, producing the hard copy which is still an essential final stage in the man-machine interface, great strides have been taken. Limitations which existed in 1980 have been overcome and – provided you are prepared to spend the money – almost anything is now possible, quality-wise, and in brilliant colour. New devices have made life easier for the non-keyboarding operator of management information systems. The touch-screen, the mouse, the light pen and the optical scanner now provide alternatives to QWERTY, with voice coming up fast. On the software side – that is, the programs that make it all possible – programs are being written which make the cheapest and most basic machines almost as friendly as the expensive 'dedicated' equipment of not so long ago. At the present time, the personal computer (PC) is enjoying an unprecedented boom. One major manufacturer claims that for his industry-standard PC on average one new program is written *every day*. In communications, cable television which will eventually provide a virtually house-to-house communications network is just beginning to stir. The UK is on the verge of introducing the '*X*' telephone network constructed specifically for data-communication. The 'ordinary' telephone system is making extensive use of advanced technology with digital exchanges, fibre-optics and microwave transmission. Computer networks are being developed which will allow any and every computer to communicate with others regardless of size, make or protocol.

In short, what we saw happening in 1980 is still happening, but more quickly, more easily, and more cheaply. Short of the 'quantum leaps' beloved of our more innovative developers, it is likely that we will see a similar – if accelerated – development over the next few years. It is already apparent that technology is outstripping our capacity to understand and use it to the full. What is now needed is a more intensive campaign to educate potential users of office technology in the benefits which can thus be achieved. We still have the two opposing forces of advancing technology versus resistance to change and there is no reason to believe that this situation will alter – it is a basic fact of human nature.

The effect on the office environment

What will be the effect of the new technology on the appearance of the office? A typist of twenty or even thirty years ago would have little difficulty in identifying a modern typewriter as such, nor would a filing-cabinet or stencil duplicator present too many problems. Will today's office worker recognise the equipment of even five years hence as easily? The typewriter as we know it will almost certainly have disappeared. The heavy, clattering chunks of machinery which cluttered the offices of the 1970s will only survive in the older offices. In modern firms they will have been replaced by slim electronic keyboards connected to VDU screens and fast, silent printing units. As typewriters become smaller and slimmer, the QWERTY keyboard will remain, like the Cheshire cat's grin in Alice in Wonderland, until it too fades and becomes redundant as man discovers more direct ways of communicating with machines.

Long before that happens, the keyboard will have become a familiar tool to a far wider range of people. Computer terminals will become commonplace on the executive's desk, assuming that he still *has* a desk in his office and assuming that he still has an *office*. The executive's work-station may become a combination of keyboard, VDU and telephone, and who is to say that this work-station needs to be located 'at the office'? The joys of commuting could be ended for many by a complete decentralisation of resources, allowing the executive to work from home.

On a strictly practical note, new technology *is* – or should be – having direct effect on the office environment as such. Increased use of VDUs means that office designers and architects are paying more attention to such things as lighting and air-conditioning. Special desks and seating built on ergonomic principles ensure the comfort of the operator. New buildings invariably have built-in trunking to carry electrical and communications services throughout, and where new internal telephone exchanges are installed, data-communications facilities are a prime consideration. The office is becoming quieter, as silent image-printers or impact-printers in acoustic cabinets take over from rattling typewriters. Press-button telephones with auto-dialling facilities speed up communication, and communicating word-processors and computers reduce internal paperwork.

Resistance to change

So, on the one hand we have a technology which could completely change the face of the office, on the other the resistance to change which has been the despair of every innovator, Organisation and Methods practitioner, office equipment salesman and management accountant since the term 'business efficiency' was coined: the same resistance to change which perpetuates the status-symbol of the secretary-nursemaid guarding the threshold of her boss's inner sanctum. Usually under-employed, her undoubted skills atrophied through disuse, her only recompense for boredom is the inflated salary she no doubt commands. The dictation machine has existed for some eighty years and yet, even in those countries where it enjoys a relatively high acceptance, saturation is nowhere near achieved, the reason being that although the machine is clearly more efficient and cost-effective than other methods, it strikes at the very heart of the boss/secretary relationship which is the corner-stone of the traditional office. In such a climate what chance is there for the word processor – except as one more status-symbol to decorate the office of the Managing-Director's secretary? Where such an attitude persists, the future is likely to bear an uncanny resemblance to the present, or to what for many forward-thinking companies is already the past.

Compromise   For most, the probable result will be a compromise somewhere in between the two extremes. Whatever the individual solution however, there is bound to be an over-all effect on the employment situation, and a reorientation of personal and social values. The use of computers in the data-processing field did not result in massive unemployment, but in a readjustment of requirements. Many boring, time-consuming jobs disappeared, but the easy availability of information and statistics made possible many new techniques in forward-planning, forecasting and marketing-model building. Similarly, the advent of word processing will create many new possibilities in the field of text. Jobs which tended to be swept under the carpet will be done because they have become easy. Mailing lists, internal directories, price lists and so on will be more easily kept up to date. Personalised mailings will be produced where previously the high cost of individually-typed letters resulted in recourse to the duplicated effort with names and addresses patched-in afterwards.

At the same time, the increase in *total* secretarial efficiency will enable it to cope with an ever-increasing workload. Falling rolls in schools and colleges will, to a certain extent, balance out redundancies caused by rationalisation, but the educational institutions will need to monitor the changing situation constantly and vigilantly. Throughput of secretarial trainees will need to be adapted to *local* demand, as far as can be ascertained. There is little to be gained by turning out hundreds of highly-trained shorthand writers when the only major employer in the area is 100 per cent audio. Similarly some effort should be made to discover the potential requirements of the future employers of our students as regards the various *grades* of word-processor operator.

More leisure   The impact of the microprocessor and its successors will not of course be restricted to the office. Better and cheaper automation of manufacturing and distribution processes will also result in reorientation of labour demands. It is likely that the worker of the future will enjoy more leisure, and this in itself may lead to new requirements in education. If leisure is to be of benefit, it should be used as an opportunity for the broadening of interests and for active participation. If we are not to become a world of passive, television-watching, button-pressing extensions of the very machines which have made our leisure possible, there must be a conscious effort to educate people to make the most of their spare time. Microelectronics itself will undoubtedly play a large part in the reorientation towards increased leisure, and the more profitable use of spare time. Developments in television-based Prestel and Teletext-type systems will, with the advent of cable television, enable 'interactive' television to become a reality. No longer will viewing be merely passive. Simple controls will enable you to 'go shopping' by videotaped display or catalogue. You will be able to call up a demonstration of new equipment for the home; a 'tour' of holiday resorts or accommodation; a fashion show in your own living room. A keyboard connected to the television will enable you to order goods for delivery to your door, and the inclusion of a credit-card number will pay for them – instantly and painlessly. If you need to know whether you can afford it, a call to your own bank's computer through a closed user-group 'gateway' will bring a copy of your bank statement to the screen. A small printer will provide a permanent record if required. For those anxious to *improve* their minds or skills, educational programmes on videotape or video disk, incorporating viewer-participation in programmed learning, will revolutionise further and higher education. No longer will it be necessary to 'go' to night school or further education classes except for practical work involving heavy or expensive equipment and materials.

Not only in the field of education will microelectronics contribute towards a fuller and more satisfying life, but in entertainment too it will play a major part. The television set will develop from the 'goggle-box' of the 1970s into an inter-active medium allowing audience-participation from the viewer's own fireside (if such an old-fashioned term is allowed to survive). The home computer has already ousted the model railway. Today's children are more likely to be found building up computer programs for sophisticated inter-active video games than bridges and cranes from Meccano. Schools introduce computers as early as the infants' classes and what to us were the marvels of electronics are marvels no more. One wonders what the next generation will consider commonplace!

Returning to the field of business, the inevitable result of computerisation of so many commercial functions will be a general speeding-up of business methods. With more and more real-time data-processing systems for ordering and despatching goods, with automated stock-control and materials handling, commerce will no more proceed at a speed dictated by an out-dated, overloaded postal system. Virtually instantaneous inter-account cash transfer will similarly speed up the fiscal system and do much to eradicate the evils of extended credit, bad debts and bouncing cheques.

The removal from the post offices of the world of countless thousands of tonnes of orders, confirmations, invoices, statements and cheques should allow those organisations to concentrate their resources upon providing an efficient service for those items which still require physical transference.

All this will not happen overnight. As was stated by the Council for Educational Technology in *Microelectronics: Their Implications for Education and Training*, as long ago as 1978, and remains valid today: 'The time-scale of change . . . shortens rapidly with the advance of technology: if indeed we are on the threshold of a new industrial revolution, it may come upon us in decades rather than centuries.'

During this transitory stage, many thousands of businesses will continue to use the methods and technologies of the present or even the past, adapting slowly and reluctantly to the new world. The pamphlet goes on to voice a caution in which many who are resistant to change may find some comfort: 'Even in a time of revolutionary change, many things remain much as they always were.' Or, as the French novelist and journalist Alphonse Karr put it, far more succinctly, long before all this was ever thought of: *'Plus ça change, plus c'est la même chose.'*

Glossary

This is a list of the more common words associated with word processing and the new technology in general. Most are also covered within the text of the book, but some have been included because, although they are not directly connected with word processing, they are likely to be found in magazine articles, etc., where word processing is discussed.

This is by no means a complete glossary of terms which you are likely to encounter in the field of information technology, but has been tailored to the approximate level of knowledge assumed in a reader of this book. A more advanced glossary of terms will be found in *Beyond Word Processing,* the companion book to this one, which covers in more detail the principles of data communication and information technology.

Access Used indiscriminately as a noun or verb. As a noun it means more or less the same as in normal usage. 'To access' means 'to gain access to' or 'to secure the use of'.

Alphanumeric Letters and numbers, usually in description of a keyboard containing both. Strictly speaking, the QWERTY keyboard is alphanumeric, but the term commonly denotes that the numeric section is arranged as on a calculator, and is used for a similar purpose.

Background A 'background' function in word processing is one which is carried out independently of the keyboard and VDU, which can then be used for something else. Printing-out, for example, may be a background function. While the word processor is printing from a disk, the operator can be using the keyboard and screen to prepare the next job.

Batch-processing When similar kinds of operation are collected together for a computer-run. If, for example, a large number of invoices have to be printed, it makes sense to batch-process, so that the computer is repeatedly using the same program, rather than interspersing with other jobs of a different kind.

Bells and whistles An American term for the features of a computer or word processor which are likely to cause an exaggerated reaction among observers of a demonstration.

Binary code The reduction of numbers to a series of 1s and 0s by expressing them to base 2.

Bit In the strings of 1s and 0s which make up the binary or digital code each 1 or 0 is termed a 'bit'.

Block-limit When editing text on the VDU, block-limits are instructions given to the CPU by positioning the cursor first at the beginning, then at the end of a block of text which is to be altered in some way – moved, indented, underscored, etc.

Bubble A type of memory which is able to retain information even after the power supply to the system has been switched off.

Buffer See **Memory.**

Byte In binary code a number of 'bits' are strung together to represent a number or character. This is known as a byte. In word processing the terms byte and character are freely interchanged in designations of memory capacity. In this case the abbreviated 'B' is used, usually in conjunction with K for Kilo or M for Mega. A memory with a capacity of 64 000 characters could be variously described as 64K characters, 64K or 64KB.

Cassette A container of magnetic tape, usually holding both supply and take-up spools.

Ceefax A television-based information service, run by the BBC. A special television set will receive such things as weather reports, sports scores and so on. It should not be confused with Viewdata, which is a business service transmitted by telephone line.

Command sequence The order in which instructions are given to a word processor by operating the keyboard.

Character string A sequence of characters defined *exactly*, including all letters, symbols and written spaces. The insertion of a hyphen, a mis-spelling, addition of punctuation or written space creates a different character string.

Configuration A selection of equipment forming a word-processing or computer system.

CPS Characters per second – a measure of the speed of a printing unit.

CPU Central Processing Unit – the computer 'brain' of the word processor.

CRT Cathode Ray Tube – a television or VDU screen.

Cursor A signal on the VDU which indicates the position of the next character to be typed. For ease of location, the horizontal position of the cursor is usually duplicated on one of the status lines.

Daisy-wheel A type of printer, or more accurately the type-element of that printer in which the characters are located at the tips of flexible arms radiating from the centre like the petals of a daisy.

Default values Parameters, such as page size, pitch and linespacing, essential to the working of the system, which are set initially by the program. Unless these are changed by the operator, the system will 'default' to these values during operation.

Digital code The reduction of all characters, commands and signals to strings of 1s and 0s so that they can be understood and used by the processor.

Discrete media Recording media which can be separately handled and stored. In a word processor, disks, floppy disks, cassettes, etc. are discrete media, the main memory is not.

Disk or disc Magnetic recording medium used on word processors, and computers. In word processor/computer terms, when used in isolation, usually refers to the hard or rigid disk of the large systems. (See **Rigid disk.**)

Disk drive The mechanism which spins the disk, reads from it, or 'writes' upon it in digital code.

Diskette See **Floppy disk.**

Dot matrix A type of printing head in which the characters are formed of dots, like the lane or speed-restriction signs on the motorway. In a 10×12 matrix there would be 120 dots in twelve horizontal lines of ten dots. These are usually high-speed printers used for computer print-out or draft-quality word processor output.

Embolden A method of producing bold type on an impact-type printer such as a daisy-wheel. The character is printed once normally, then after a fractional shift to the right, is printed again, making the impression thicker and darker than usual.

Facsimile transmission A means of transmitting a facsimile copy of document or drawing over a telephone line. The original is scanned by the transmitting machine, the image is converted into digital or audio signals, and these are decoded by the receiving instrument which converts them back into hard copy.

Fax Short for facsimile transmission.

Floppy disk A disk of flexible plastic material, faced on one or both sides with magnetic material, used for storing information in the form of digital code. Most carry around 300K characters – about 130 A4 pages of typing. Otherwise known as **flexible disk** or **diskette.**

Format The arrangement, or layout of the printed page. Covers such things as margins, tabs, alignment.

Global replace The ability of a word processor to search an entire document for a specified 'character-string' and wherever it occurs, to replace it with another.

Glossary The ability to produce an index of given words with the page-numbers on which they occur. Some manufacturers use this to describe a 'dictionary' program for checking correct spelling.

Graphics A feature available on some word processors which enables the operator to draw horizontal or vertical lines on the VDU. May be used to produce organisation or flow-charts, or to rule up forms. Graphics on a computer is the ability to represent facts, statistics, figures in non-text form, such as graphs, bar-charts, pie-charts etc., often in three-dimensional form.

Half-tone An effect used on the VDU screen to highlight characters which are to be the subject of some further operation such as underlining or moving. The characters appear against an illuminated background. This has less brightness than the characters themselves, so they can still be read.

Hard copy Any form of finished document which can be read, transported and stored – as distinct from the image on a VDU, or a recording on magnetic media.

Hardwired Be careful with this one! It appears to be used in more than one sense. To one person it may mean that a piece of equipment is literally connected together by using wire or cable as distinct from printed circuit boards: to another it indicates that the equipment is pre-programmed, and that the programme cannot be changed. If in any doubt, do not hesitate to ask anybody using this – or for that matter any other 'buzzword' – what exactly he or she means. You will often find that such terms are quite incorrectly used.

Indexing In dictation equipment, the production of a slip of paper, or by other means indicating to the transcribing typist the length of each letter, and the location of special instructions.

Ink-jet printer A printing unit which operates by squirting ink at the paper in the form of the characters instead of producing them by impact, as on a typewriter or daisy-wheel printer.

Interface Used as a noun, 'interface' means something, usually electronic but not necessarily so by definition, which allows one piece of equipment to work with another. For example, in a centralised dictation system, a dictation recording machine may be controlled by dialling numbers on a telephone. The interface changes the pulses generated by the dial into signals which can be recognised by the recorder. In simple terms, think of an interface as an adapter.

You sometimes hear 'interface' used as a term in human relations. A meeting for example may be referred to as 'a useful interface between departments'. Used in this sense it probably means 'liaison' which might perhaps have been a better word in the first place.

As a verb, 'to interface' means 'to work with', or 'to act as an interface between'.

Justify Produce a straight-line right hand margin, as on a printed page. This takes effect during the printing operation. The justified margin may or may not appear on the VDU.

K Short for Kilo – a thousand.

Kilobyte A thousand bytes – or in word-processing terms, characters.

Laser A narrow beam of high-intensity light, used for many purposes. In a high-energy form it is used in engineering for cutting, welding, piercing and forming operations. In surgery it is used for cauterising wounds, or destroying unwanted tissue. In office equipment it is usually found in a low-energy form, and is used in conjunction with optical fibres in communications. In video-disk and audio-disk recording and playback, the laser beam replaces the stylus of a conventional record-player.

LCD Liquid Crystal Display. A type of display of letters or figures, used on pocket calculators or digital watches. Often used as a display on electronic typewriters, and at the time of writing has just begun to emerge as a display medium for portable computers. Shows as dark characters on a light-coloured background.

LED Light-emitting Diode. In effect a small light bulb, but using far less current than a filament lamp. Increasingly used for 'pilot' and indicator lights on all kinds of electronic equipment.

Library In word processing, where a number of long or difficult words or phrases are used repeatedly, they can be stored in a special memory and called forth as required by keying in a simple code. For example, keying in 'WP' could be made to produce the words 'word processing'.

Line-printer A kind of printer which prints out a whole line at once, at a very high speed. The quality of such printing is not good enough for word-processing copy, but may be used for producing rough drafts for subsequent editing and retyping.

M Mega – a million.

Mainframe A large computer. In word-processing terms, usually one which is already being used for data processing, stock-control, etc., but which can be 'accessed' by a word-processing terminal consisting simply of a keyboard and VDU. The mainframe computer in this case replaces the CPU of the stand-alone configuration.

Megabyte A million bytes, or characters.

Memory The measure of the 'power' or ability of the word processor is the size of its memory – how many bytes, or characters, can be stored and recalled for use.

A word processor may have several memories of different kinds. The *Main Memory*, which is the one usually quoted in the advertisements, holds the information which is currently in use – the program, and the page which is displayed on the screen, for example. Other information which may be needed is contained in the disk storage, and can be called forth as required.

In addition there may be other short-term memories.

The memory is contained in a series of silicon chips, or microprocessors, and these can be of three basic types:

ROM Read Only Memory. In this type, the program is built-in and cannot be changed. It is used in pocket calculators, television games and similar applications, and in the very simple word processors which are only programmed to perform a limited number of functions.

PROM   Programmable Read Only Memory. The program is fed into the micro-
        processor after it is manufactured. It is possible to 'bleach-out' or erase a
        program by the use of ultra-violet light, and feed in a different program; but this
        can only be done by the manufacturer, not the user.

RAM   Random Access Memory. This is the most versatile. The RAM is programmed
        by the user every time the machine is switched on, by running a 'program disk' or
        tape. The same machine can therefore perform many different tasks, according to
        the program currently in use. Special 'software packages' or programs can be
        obtained to offer such facilities as 'SORT AND MERGE' or mathematical
        functions. The use of RAM also means that a machine is not outdated by its
        program, as it can be updated by the use of more advanced software.

Buffer, scratch   These are small, short-term memories, or parts of the main memory, used for
pad or putaside   things like moving text from one page to another, or calling up frequently used
        terms from a Library.

Merge   The ability to use information from two or more memories or stores to produce a
        composite document. For example, a mailing list of names and addresses on one
        disk can be merged with a standard letter on another to produce personalised
        mailings. Information may be merged from different combinations of sources:
        from two work disks in separate disk drives, from the main memory and a work
        disk, from the main memory and the 'putaside' memory, and so on. It is usually
        taken to refer to drawing information from two work disks or similar storage
        media simultaneously.

Microcassette   A small cassette used in some dictation systems and for data-storage. Care is
        needed here to avoid confusion with the Mini-cassette, which is similar in size
        and is also used in dictation systems, data processing and some simple
        word-processing machines. To add to the confusion, the terms are occasionally
        misused even by manufacturers. The tape-drive principles are entirely different,
        and the two are in no way interchangeable. The easiest way of differentiating
        between them is to look at the holes in the centre of the spools. The microcassette
        has holes resembling those in the familiar C-type compact cassette. The holes in
        the Mini-cassette have the shape of a six-pointed star.

Microprocessor   The 'chip'. The silicon chip which contains the memory. May be of the various
        types described under **Memory** and may be used singly or connected together in
        multiples to increase the capacity of the memory.

Mini-cassette   A small cassette measuring approx. 55mm × 35mm used in many dictation
        systems, data-processing systems, minicomputers and editing typewriters.

Mnemonic   The use of letters or words on the normal QWERTY keyboard to give
        'commands' or instructions to a word processor instead of having special keys
        for every one, for instance L = Line, P = Paragraph, J = Justify, C = Centre and
        so on.

Mode   Defines the *type* of operation which a word processor may be required to
        perform, such as Mode Locate, Mode Capitals, etc. Modes can be divided into

two types, those which govern the operation of the machine, such as Print, Locate, Define, Graphics, etc., and those which have secondary characteristics such as Capitals, Underline, Sub- and Superscript, Align and Insert.

Monitor As a noun, a 'monitor' is usually a television screen which exists for the purpose of checking upon the progress of an activity, or a state of affairs. For example, a monitor in a television studio is there for the benefit of the technicians, whereas a similar set in the home would be for entertainment.

As a verb, 'to monitor' means to oversee, or keep a check upon, for example, 'to monitor the progress of a patient'.

Narrow-window A type of text display on an editing typewriter or elementary word processor which contains only a single line of text.

OCR Optical Character Recognition. By using a special typeface known as OCR-font, text can be produced which, while retaining its normal form to the extent that it can still be read, is also recognisable to a machine. Everyday examples can be seen on cheque books, credit cards, and similar documents which are processed by machine.

Off-line An operation in word processing which is performed by a piece of equipment working alone – that is, not connected to a computer or CPU. An off-line printer, for example, would be a self-contained unit printing from disks or other discrete media which had been prepared on another machine.

On-line Opposite to 'off-line' – a piece of equipment or operation which is dependent upon other equipment, and connected by cable. A computer terminal is said to be 'on-line' to the main computer or CPU.

Optical fibres Fine strands of high-quality glass, along which light can be made to travel just as electricity flows along a wire. They can be bent around corners, or fed through conduits without loss of continuity. Electrical signals such as digital code or voice-produced modulations are converted into light at their source, transmitted along the optical fibres with very little loss of strength, and reconverted into electricity at the receiving end. One advantage is that they cannot be tapped or intercepted on the way, and so make for a secure communications system. Optical fibres are fast replacing copper wire in the telephone network.

Opto-electronics The science of combining optics with electronics by such means as lasers, light-emitting diodes and optical fibres.

Oracle A television-based information service run by the Independent Broadcasting Authority. Like Ceefax (run by the BBC) it should not be confused with Viewdata.

PABX Private Automatic Branch Exchange. The internal telephone system which is also connected through Post Office or telephone company wiring to the main exchange.

Paginate To allot sequential numbers to the pages of a book or document. Alternatively in word processing, to allot an equal number of lines to each page of a multi-page document.

PAX Private Automatic Exchange. The internal telephone system which is *not* connected to the outside world through the main exchange, and exists solely for internal communication.

Peripherals Pieces of equipment designed to work with, but not connected to, a word processor or computer, for example OCR reader, or paper-tape punch.

Prestel In Britain, the Post Office service which allows the transmission of television-based information via telephone lines. See also **Viewdata**.

PROM Programmable Read Only Memory. See **Memory**.

Prompt A message which appears on one of the status lines of a VDU in the form of either a question or instruction. Its purpose is either to inform the operator, or to guide her through a 'command sequence'.

Putaside The temporary storing of a block of text in a special memory. It can be used for moving text from one page or another, storing and recalling vocabulary terms or 'Define Strings', or overlaying graphics with characters with graphics.

QWERTY The standard typewriter keyboard – so called from the arrangement of the first keys on the top row. Devised by Christopher Sholes in 1873 in a deliberate attempt to slow down the operator to prevent jamming of the typebars.

RAM Random Access Memory. See **Memory**.

Random-access The ability to go straight to a piece of information or data stored in a computer or word processor, as is possible when using disk or magnetic card. The opposite of **Sequential Access.**

Rigid disk A storage medium used mainly on large computers and shared-logic word processors. So called to distinguish it from the floppy disk used on smaller systems.

ROM Read Only Memory. See **Memory**.

Scratch pad A short-term memory. See **Memory**.

Screen-based An operation requiring the use of the VDU screen. Alternatively, a system which employs a VDU.

Scrolling If you think of the VDU screen as a window through which you can see only part of a document, perhaps only the top half of the page or four out of six columns, 'scrolling' in effect 'moves' the document up and down, or sideways, so that the remainder may be seen.

Search and replace The ability of a word processor to search for a specified character-string, that is a word or phrase, throughout the length of a document, and each time it occurs to replace it with another specified character-string.

Sequential access   The need, when searching for information in a store or memory, to go through all the stored information in sequence until the required portion is reached. This happens when magnetic tape is used as a storage medium, and is the reason that cassette-based systems are much slower than disk. Opposite of **Random Access.**

Shared-logic   A system in which the central processor, or computer, is shared by more than one operator, each having her own keyboard and video display.

Software   The program of a computer or word processor, as opposed to the equipment, which is known as the 'hardware'. A word processor using random-access memory, which needs to be programmed each time it is used, is often referred to as being 'software-based'.

Sort   The ability of a word processor to sort information keyed-in at random into alphabetical or numerical order.

Stand-alone   A word-processing system which is self-contained, having its own CPU, as opposed to shared-logic or mainframe systems where the processor is shared between two or more terminals.

Status line   A line on a VDU screen which contains information relevant to the work being carried out. There may be several status lines, containing such information as page size and length, margin and tab settings, the programme in use, the 'mode' of operation in use, and so on.

Stop code   A signal inserted into a text, which causes the printer to stop at predetermined places perhaps in order for the operator to insert variables, or simply because the end of a page has been reached.

String-search   A 'string' is a set of characters making up a word or phrase. A word processor can be instructed to search for a specified 'string' or character-set throughout a whole document and either erase it or replace it with something else each time it occurs.

Switch-code   A signal – usually producing a distinctive identifying symbol on the VDU screen, which acts as an instruction to the printing unit. A switch-code may, for example, instruct the printer to indent a paragraph, or justify the right-hand margin.

Tape-punch   A machine which produces punched paper tape for use in a Telex machine or phototypesetter. Tape-punches may be used as peripherals to a word-processing system.

Thin-window   A display showing only one line of text.

Tractor-feed   A device attached to the printing unit of a word processor to enable continuous stationery to be used.

User-friendly An American term indicating that a machine is easy to operate, or designed with the user in mind. Such machines may be programmed to interrogate, or lead the operator through complicated command sequences. Other contributions towards 'user-friendliness' may include the use of plain-language commands or mnemonics.

VDU Video (or Visual) Display Unit. The 'television screen' used to display text or data on a word processor or computer.

Viewdata The transmission of informative material along telephone lines for display on a television set. Any subscriber who has the necessary equipment can call up information on business matters, the Stock Exchange, travel, employment and so on.

Word-wraparound On a word processor, when a matter is to be inserted, the text displayed on the VDU drops down a line to leave room for the new matter. When the operation has been completed, the remainder of the text readjusts itself to follow on from the insertion. Similarly, if matter is deleted, the remaining text closes up, drawing words from the next and succeeding lines as necessary to produce an unbroken line of text.

Index